I0879605

A LITERARY FIELD GUIDE TO NORTHERN APPALACHIA

The bigger, fiercer, wilder relative of the Sharp-
short, broad wings and a long rudderlike tail that give
superb aerial agility. These secretive birds are mostly
flash through forests
and mammal prey,
pouncing silently
first through brush
grab quarry in
Falconers have
trained goshawks
thousand years
pairs build and maintain
options available, they
year after
year, or may switch to a
add fresh conifer needles
Aromatic chemicals in
natural insecticide and
well known for its
alternate short flights
as they search for prey,
quickly and silently,
reckless hunters fly at high
occasionally stalk prey on foot
capture mammals more than
sky dance as part of their
fly together in an undulating
vocal when defending their
human intruders and kill
including owls and hawks.
finding a Northern Goshawk is
mature forest being as quiet,
In some years, perhaps when
north, autumn invasions may
short bursts of amazingly fast
among branches and crashing
the intensity of pursuit.
found in both deciduous and
normally only vocalize during
always found solitarily or

A Literary Field Guide to Northern Appalachia

Edited by Todd Davis and Noah Davis

Carolyn G. Mahan, NATURAL HISTORY EDITOR

The University of Georgia Press — Athens

A Wormsloe
FOUNDATION
nature book

© 2024 by the University of Georgia Press
Athens, Georgia 30602
www.ugapress.org
All rights reserved
Designed by Erin Kirk
Set in Arno Pro
Printed and bound by Sheridan Books
The paper in this book meets the guidelines for permanence and durability of the Committee on Production Guidelines for Book Longevity of the Council on Library Resources.

Most University of Georgia Press titles are available from popular e-book vendors.

Printed in the United States of America
28 27 26 25 24 C 5 4 3 2 1

Library of Congress Cataloging-in-Publication Data

Names: Davis, Todd F., 1965– editor. | Davis, Noah (Poet), editor. | Mahan, Carolyn G., editor.
Title: A literary field guide to northern Appalachia / edited by Todd Davis and Noah Davis ; Carolyn G. Mahan, Natural history editor.
Description: Athens : The University of Georgia Press, [2024]. | Includes bibliographical references.
Identifiers: LCCN 2024013163 | ISBN 9780820367422 (hardback) | ISBN 9780820367514 (epub) | ISBN 9780820367521 (pdf)
Subjects: LCSH: Nature—Poetry. | Natural history—Appalachian Region—Poetry. | American poetry—21st century.
Classification: LCC PS310.N3 L575 2024 | DDC 811/.6080360974—dc23/eng/20240521

LC record available at https://lccn.loc.gov/2024013163

Contents

VII — INVERTEBRATES

VIII — FUNGI

Acknowledgments

— We'd like to thank our families—Kurt, Carl, and Clare Engstrom; Shelly and Nathan Davis; and Nikea Ulrich—for their support over the years as they've watched us pursue our passion for the greater-than-human natural world.

We give thanks for the public lands of the Northern Appalachians and for the private landowners who are good stewards of their properties in this region.

We also offer thanks for the rich biodiversity of the Northern Appalachians and pray that we learn to care for it better.

Thanks, too, to our fellow faculty and students in the Environmental Studies Program at Penn State Altoona and colleagues in the Theodore Roosevelt Conservation Partnership.

We acknowledge our debt to the many researchers, naturalists, and scholars, past and present, who have built the foundation of scientific discovery upon which this book is built.

Finally, much of this work was helped along the way by grants and a sabbatical from the Pennsylvania State University. We thank the university for its support.

A LITERARY FIELD GUIDE TO NORTHERN APPALACHIA

Editor's Introduction

— How does a field guide help guide a person into a place, into the living, complex system of, say, a streambed in a northern hardwood forest? How best to introduce another living being, another species and all it holds and beholds, to a person who may not have known or even heard of that living being before?

As so many naturalists and eco-thinkers, so many ecologists and environmentalists have suggested, have pleaded, have shouted and implored, we must heal the divorce of our species from all other species, mend the rift, and reestablish relationships with the world that sustains us, that makes our very lives possible.

At the headwaters of finding a way back to this relationship, I'd argue, are love, wonder, and awe, all of which blossom as one nurtures a more intimate knowledge of other life-forms. If we're to back away from the precipice of extinction and the despoilation of the planet in the twenty-first century, we need to listen to the trees and plants, to attend to birds in the air and fish in the streams. We need to follow the paths animals follow, to learn how they live in concert with their surroundings. These creatures are our kin and we theirs, as Native peoples have taught for thousands of years—and as science continues to demonstrate with studies that show the dramatic percentage of DNA we share. But, sadly, like a dysfunctional family, more and more of us know less and less about the other lives that populate our home ground, threatening biodiversity and the stability and health of ecosystems.

The act of naming can be a way of developing relationships, a possible demonstration of affection and care for these other living beings. Most of us who move through the consumer world can name countless apps and stores, musical groups and actors, brands of clothing and kitchen appliances, cars and beverages and deodorants and shampoos and and and . . .

But if we're asked to name a tree or flower as we walk a path in the forest, to identify the track of some mammal or its scat, a butterfly or bird that floats over our head, we likely come up blank and stammering, perhaps even equivocating that it's impossible to know the names of so many creatures.

While recognizing and naming and learning more about the life cycles of certain creatures are small acts that must begin with rudimentary steps—like learning the names and characteristics of a few of the living creatures that live in the air around us or in the ground at our feet or in the water we drink or irrigate our crops with—it's a crucial movement toward what botanist Robin Wall Kimmerer, an enrolled member of the Citizen Potawatomi, has called gratitude and reciprocity in her wise book *Braiding Sweetgrass.*

The more-than-human natural world is not an abstract concept. We cannot love and care for abstractions. It is in the particular, in the individual, that we find expression, the possibility of relationship. And relationship demands we listen and learn, that we start to grow in our knowledge of that individual living creature. "Attention is the beginning of devotion," Mary Oliver writes, and I might add that there is no respect, there is no love, without a desire to know another more deeply.

I grew up in a household where field guides made regular appearances, pulled out over a dinner conversation or from a rucksack on a hike. But my true connection to certain flowers and trees—like the sugar maple that was struck by lightning and wept sap one February, a tree I visited each morning for several weeks to lick the frozen slick of sugar—came about through story and image and touch, the engagement of the five senses in art and science and experience.

A Literary Field Guide to Northern Appalachia, which is a continuation of the work begun by Rose McLarney, Laura-Gray Street, and L. L. Gaddy in their beautiful and insightful *A Literary Field Guide to Southern Appalachia,* should not be misconstrued as a replacement for more traditional field guides. Carolyn G. Mahan, Noah Davis, and I have shelves of field guides that we return to in our offices or carry into the field. We love how each performs in different, idiosyncratic ways, how they help us see bishop's cap or fringed polygala after identifying the plant along the stream where we've hiked. Field guides are a work of devotion and wonder, of natural science and taxonomy; dwelling for a time within their pages can lead to a deeper perception, a more profound empathy, for the elaborate intricacy of the webbing of the world we live in and are a part of.

What *A Literary Field Guide to Northern Appalachia* recognizes and celebrates is the fact that humans are storytelling creatures who like to sing in poems, who compose in order to remember and to grow closer to what they have come into contact with. And like those earliest humans, we also draw, perhaps not on a cave wall but on boxcars and the sides of buildings, on fine parchment and wood; we draw so we can see again what has dazzled us or confused us or frightened us or simply astounded us with its very existence.

This book sets out to introduce the reader to seventy particular species found in Northern Appalachia, a region comprised of parts of Ohio, Pennsylvania, New York, Connecticut, New Jersey, Massachusetts, Vermont, New Hampshire, and Maine. This book is a celebration of different life-forms in the region, a party of sorts where we hope the reader will metaphorically shake hands with and greet the flowers and trees and shrubs and mammals and birds and amphibians and reptiles and fish and invertebrates and fungi that reside along the spine of the Appalachian Mountains, in its valleys and watersheds.

There are millions of species in the region and selecting only seventy was not only difficult but painful. How many of our favorites are not included here! But like any good party, this is just a foretaste, something to whet the appetite of curiosity. Wouldn't it be wonderful if the readers of this book would begin to make entries of their own to share with family members or friends, to help them remember and understand better their encounters with other species on their home ground?

The brief introductions in this book—encounters that we hope will tug the reader into deeper study and relationship—include a natural history and ecological description written by biologists who have given their professional life (and sometimes their personal life) over to the living beings in that particular taxonomy, studying them, caring about and for them. Each entry also invites a poet to "sing" about the species, to weave a story, to offer a metaphor that will help us understand and remember a little better, a little longer, to begin a relationship that might last a lifetime or more, as this love or admiration might be passed onto someone else. And, finally, each entry provides a drawing, an illustrative interpretation of the species, framed by an artist who has pondered perspective and line, shading and white space, bringing some aspect of the species to life on the page, as only visual artists can do.

We hope what is foregrounded in this book is the plant or animal, the living creature the page is devoted to. While humans do walk among these pages, we wanted more than anything for the living beings who have been neglected, who have been desecrated and threatened by industrialization, extraction, and overconsumption, to take center stage. After all, it's about getting to know them, asking forgiveness and permission to learn from them so they might show us a way forward.

Todd Davis

— I write this introduction from the limestone Nittany Valley in the Ridge and Valley province of Pennsylvania. Todd Davis, my coeditor and friend, lives one valley west, tucked against the North America continental plate that forms the eastern-most edge of the Appalachian Plateau. The Appalachian Plateau, Ridge and Valley, and New England constitute the geomorphological provinces of Northern Appalachia. These provinces, defined by their underlying rocks and geologic history, create the foundation in terms of elevation, soil, and vegetation of the Northern Appalachian Mountains.

These ancient mountains, covered with expansive forests, once formed the great eastern wilderness, home to numerous tribal groups, including the Susquehannock and the Haudenosaunee, among others. The past four hundred years of European colonization and American industrialization have profoundly shaped the ecologies we know today, which many of the poems in this book address. The landscape of the Northern Appalachians and its flora and fauna, including the introduction of many species from other parts of the world, changed dramatically with the establishment of canals, railroads, and roads by the mid-1800s.

This morning in mid-April a house wren, newly arrived from the south, sings in our blooming hawthorn tree. Other neotropical migratory birds are beginning to arrive. Soon, jewel-colored warblers, spotted-breasted thrushes, and tiny hummingbirds will pour into the region. These species spend their winters in the tropics but migrate north along the Appalachian spine to breed and raise their young in these forests. That should give you a sense of the richness of the Appalachian landscape—birds leave the most diverse ecosystem in the world (the tropical rainforest) to nest here. Their stay will be short. By early August, the migratory birds will begin their journey back south.

These yearly cycles are a hallmark of the Appalachians with natural events marking each month and season. The call of spring peepers, peenting woodcock, and blooming skunk cabbage mark the beginning of spring in my valley, even if snow and ice still cover the ground. Fireflies—including the remarkable synchronous firefly (*Photinus carolinus*)—brighten the short nights of the summer solstice. Goldenrods and asters blanket old fields in September and give way to the famous colors of autumn foliage. Winter arrives and is quiet. Snow covers the mountains, black bears hibernate, deer seek shelter in the laurel thickets, and chickadees and nuthatches—hardy, resident birds—forage in mixed flocks.

For more than twenty-five years, I have taught students about this amazing landscape and shown them that in Appalachia you find nature everywhere. Even at my home, located near a busy downtown, big brown bats roost behind our porch broom, Carolina wrens nest in the window box, and red squirrels store black walnuts in our walls.

Three ideas dominate my lessons about these mountains. The Appalachians are diverse. The Appalachians are ancient. The Appalachians are resilient.

Geologic features of the Appalachians were born 300 million years ago when the North America continental plate was located near the equator and supported immense coal swamp forests that, over time, became the rich coal, oil, and natural gas fields of the Appalachians. The landscape was changed dramatically by the Appalachian orogeny, a mountain-building event caused by the collision of the Africa and North America tectonic plates 250 million years ago. The resulting mountains rivaled the present-day Himalayans in their scale and elevation. Over the next 200 million years, these mountains eroded to their current height and form. The highest peaks in Northern Appalachia today are about sixty-five hundred feet in elevation. The characteristic steep valleys and mountain ravines are further evidence of the Appalachians' age. An old landscape is dominated by rivers and streams, not ponds and lakes, although the last ice age did carve glacial lakes and kettle ponds into the northern regions of this ancient landscape.

The hundreds of millions of years of history of the Appalachians provided the time necessary for new species to evolve through natural selection and adaptation to local environments and landscapes. Because of this evolutionary history, native and endemic plants (serviceberry), vertebrates (brook trout), and invertebrates (eastern elliptio mussel) dot the Appalachians—species you can read about in this book.

Another contributing factor to the biodiverse landscape is the reliable presence of water. The Appalachian Mountains have a precipitation regime that is constant year-round and, therefore, supports forests, maintains stream flows, and fills aquifers. Water is a limiting factor in many global ecosystems (e.g., prairies, deserts), but the Appalachian snows, rains, and fog permit plants, fungi, invertebrates, and vertebrates to thrive. Water also contributes to the weathering and erosion of the ancient mountains, exposing differing layers of rock (e.g., limestone, sandstone, shales) and associated soil profiles. Each soil type, in turn, supports distinct floral communities.

Northern Appalachia is primarily a landscape of expansive mixed-deciduous forest. The deep soils formed from the millennia of erosion and ample rainfall ensure this woody growth. Forest communities include northern hardwoods and mixed coniferous forests on the Appalachian Plateau and higher ridges. Oak-hickory forests (and, once, American chestnut forests) dominate the well-drained soils of the eastern-most ridges. Hemlocks, beeches, and yellow birch line the steep ravines. Each forest type supports a unique assemblage of understory plants, fungi species, and associated animal communities.

As noted earlier, a characteristic trait of the Appalachians is their resilience. Born of a cataclysmic, orogeny event, the Appalachians continue to withstand natural and human-caused disturbances that have altered but not eliminated their biodiverse character. The last global ice age covered the Appalachians from northern Pennsylvania to Maine with two-mile-high glaciers that created peri-glacial environments to the south and caused the extirpation of species to the north. However, once the glaciers receded ten thousand years ago, the north–south orientation of the Appalachian Mountains permitted a rapid recolonization of the landscape by plants, vertebrates, invertebrates, and fungi that persisted in more southern regions. The mountains' north–south orientation also intercepts the prevailing winds, which contribute to thermal updrafts that facilitate the migratory pathways for birds, bats, and even monarch butterflies.

The vegetation diversity of the Appalachians is further amplified by regular, seasonal disturbances that create early successional habitats that appear and disappear on the landscape. For example, summer tornadoes on the Appalachian Plateau, microbursts, and thunderstorms with associated high winds topple forests and permit meadows, scrub habitat, and young forests to appear. Ice storms, rock falls, ridgetop wildfires, and scouring floods also periodically remove large trees, allowing forbs, grasses, shrubs, and heaths to take their place.

The Meadowcroft Rockshelter, located in western Pennsylvania, indicates that humans have inhabited the Appalachians for at least sixteen thousand years. These Indigenous peoples gave rise to the great Native tribes of Northern Appalachia: the Susquehannock, Shawnee, Iroquois, Lenape, Mohican, Abenaki, Penobscot, and others. These people inhabited a landscape dominated by old-growth forests containing 150-foot-tall white pines and hemlocks on the Appalachian Plateau and 100-foot (10-foot-diameter) oaks, hickories, and chestnuts on the southern ridges. Native Americans shaped the landscape through their use of fire, hunting, and settlement patterns. However, it was the European's ax and, later, chainsaw that removed the virgin timber. At present, the forests in our mountains are second- or even third-growth trees. The clear-cutting of forests and market hunting of the 1800s also resulted in the extirpation of mountain lions, gray wolves, and passenger pigeons from these mountains.

The Appalachians' resilience has permitted the landscape to survive the recent human disturbances of mining, fracking, and quarrying. The Appalachian landscape is an industrial landscape. Often a walk through the forest will uncover the remains of these past industries. Ironworks, charcoal flats, narrow-gauge railroads, abandoned coal mines, and acid mine drainage are all evidence of human-based disturbance. Yet still the mountains and the forests endure.

Today, nonnative pathogens (e.g., West Nile virus, chronic wasting disease, white-nose syndrome), invasive plants (e.g., Japanese knotweed), and exotic insects (e.g., gypsy moth, spotted lanternfly, emerald ash borer) imperil the Northern Appalachians and may be the most formidable threats to date. Yet we are not without hope that these natural communities might still endure. For example, researchers recently learned that a fungus native to the Appalachians is lethal to the invasive spotted lanternfly and our native mice quickly learned to devour the larva of gypsy moths. Our deep limestone caves provide protection for bats from white-nose syndrome and some bird species (e.g., American robin, northern cardinal) may develop resistance to West Nile virus.

I love these mountains and marvel at their resilience and their beauty. The beauty inspires poets, artists, and scientists. I hope that this book will give you, the reader, an opportunity to appreciate the landscape and species of Northern Appalachia in new ways. Savor each entry. Reflect on the million-year evolutionary history each entry represents. Discover the nature around you.

Carolyn G. Mahan

I — Trees and Shrubs

Allegheny Serviceberry *Amelanchier laevis*

HABITAT AND RANGE: Allegheny serviceberry is found in woods and wood margins on variable soil. This species is most abundant in the northeast, but its range extends west to Michigan and Minnesota around the Great Lakes into southern Canada and south to northern Georgia.

DESCRIPTION AND NOTES: Allegheny serviceberry is a shrub or small tree that can grow up to forty feet tall. Pinnately veined, hairless leaves are darker green above and lighter green below. Secondary veins are semicraspedodromous, meaning the vein branches near the margin with one branch forming a loop to meet the next secondary vein and the other branch terminates at the margin. Leaf margins are lined with fine sawlike teeth. At both the beginning and the end of the growing season, leaves are often purple to bronze colored. Allegheny serviceberry, a member of the rose family (Rosaceae), produces showy white flowers in the early spring. They are followed by dark purple (to red) juicy fruits in June. Fruits are sweet and were a food source for various Northern Appalachian Native Americans. Species of *Amelanchier* can often reproduce asexually, and polyploid (three or more copies of the chromosomes) individuals are common, in part due to frequent hybridization. As a result, it can be difficult to distinguish the various species of *Amelanchier*. However, diploid (two copies of the chromosomes, as typical) individuals of Allegheny serviceberry formed a discrete group in a recent study. Allegheny serviceberry may be most closely related to *Amelanchier arborea* (common serviceberry) and *Amelanchier canadensis* (Canadian serviceberry), but work to unravel the relationships of this group of plants is ongoing.

— *Neil Shepard*

Serviceberry

As shad push upstream toward spawning ground,
the first white clusters thrash and tremble
in northern wind: blossoms of shadberry
break the uniform grayness of these forests,
break the dormancy of trees still stunned
from winter: no flagging in their fluttering
white blossoms that match April's snow-
drops pushing up from snow-melt soil.

Together they bloom whiteness
erasing the last drifts of winter:
bloom even as spent shad drift
downstream, back toward the sea,
where they're snared by striped bass
or fishing nets.
                                        Centuries past,
their numbers were pure astonishment,
so vast they fed the nation's founders . . . all
long ago, as when shadberry lived
by another name, *serviceberry*,
so called because in winters past
when folks died and ground resisted
the shovel's bite, they'd keep
the body in cold storage and wait
till shad's first fluttering semaphore—
ground thawed—then dig the grave
and lay the body in, say the service
that sent them on their way
to replenish the earth.

Months from now, service-
berries will ripen, cedar waxwings
will flock amidst the limbs, open and
close their beaks on these red globes
containing sugar and sun enough
to feed their nesting season . . .
replenish their fall migration . . .

leaving behind this tree timed
to the shad's first run upstream, timed
to the last snowdrifts on the north side
of mossed birch and cedar, timed
to bloom as ground thaws,
soil opening to warmer air
that quickens the transformation
of things sloughed off by winter.

HABITAT AND RANGE: American beech is found in woods and can tolerate shade and a wide variety of soil types. Beech are found growing on acidic, loamy, moist, sandy, silty loam, well-drained, and clay soils. The range includes much of eastern North America from southern Canada south into Florida and west to Wisconsin and Texas.

DESCRIPTION AND NOTES: American beech is a large attractive tree that is frequently planted as an ornamental. It has wide, spreading branches and smooth, dull gray bark. Please resist the urge to carve your initials into its bark so that others can enjoy its beauty. American beech has simple, alternate, thin-textured leaves that are darker green above and paler green below. Venation is pinnate with evenly spaced, parallel secondaries that end at the margin in the teeth (craspedodromous). The teeth are often rather subtle, and the leaves can be slightly asymmetrical in width. Fall foliage is yellow to coppery in color. Leaves wither but often remain on the tree all winter; this type of leaf duration, termed marcescent, is common in members of Fagaceae (beech or oak family). Springtime flowers are unisexual, inconspicuous, and pollinated by the wind. Each fertilized female flower develops into a three-sided nut that is surrounded by a four-segmented spiny husk. American beech supports a wide range of wildlife, including numerous species of Lepidoptera that feed on the foliage. Various birds and mammals eat the protein-rich nuts. American beech is a timber source and has been used for furniture and flooring. Beech trees feature prominently in Middle Earth, the setting of some of the writings of J. R. R. Tolkien, including *The Hobbit* and *The Lord of the Rings*.

— *Joe Wilkins*

The Book of the American Beech

with selections from Shakespeare, Maximilian of Wied, Audubon,
and Donald Culross Peattie

Sturdy, smooth, and shining, shallow-rooted,
the fluted bole rising to *lofty crowns, the finest*
tree to be seen, the vast, late-successional woods
of American beech were for the hungers in us
long ago cut and plowed under, for the beech *loves*
what the farmer loves, rich limestone overlain
by deep, level, dark loams. Yes, what once covered

the better part of five states—*the most splendid*
forests, a most refreshing shade—is gone,
as is the passenger pigeon *to which the beech*
played lavish host, the sky-darkening flocks,
the flapping of their wings a noise like the roar
of thunder, on the hunt for beechnuts, the yearly
and unpredictable mast. At night the pigeons
roosted sometimes so thickly *the perches gave*
way under the weight, tailing to ground. Together
they fell, bird and tree, and can you imagine it
in the book of your mind? Can you write
anything so fantastic, so worthy of shining? Book,
from the Anglo-Saxon boc, *meaning a letter*
or character, from the Anglo-Saxon beece,
for beech, this is the book of the American beech,
the skin-like bark—*elegant clear gray*—arrowed
and hearted and with all our names inscribed—
O Rosalind! These trees shall be my books—
the great trunk unfurrowed, generously mossed
and lichened, and each limb down-sweeping,
each October leaf *a soft, clear yellow* and held
long into winter, even into spring, a tongue
from light to dark translated. That dark season
we were away from one another, no common
language, no custom or map, I took to wandering
the young, weedy forests of the North Country
and lost *in fable and fact,* overtaken by the dark,
reckoned the candles they were, the flames. I mean
to say more than I found my way home by reading
the book of what was—*luminous and stately tree*—
by the light thank god of beech leaves.

Balsam Fir *Abies balsamea*

HABITAT AND RANGE: This conifer prefers cool temperatures and moist soils and is common in forests and wetland edges. It is found in the northeast United States and the eastern portion of southern Canada. Its range extends west through the Great Lakes region to Minnesota. In the southern portion of its range, in Virginia and West Virginia, balsam fir is restricted to higher elevations.

DESCRIPTION AND NOTES: Balsam fir is a member of the pine family (Pinaceae) and is the only fir native to northeastern North America. These evergreen trees can grow up to eighty feet tall and are typically cone shaped with the lowermost branches touching the ground or nearly so. The branches grow off the main stem at close to perpendicular. Bark is medium gray and smooth to somewhat scaly. In addition to the overall shape of the tree, its needles provide some of the best clues that it is a fir rather than a related conifer like spruce or pine. Needles are short (usually less than one inch) with a rounded base, appear dark green in color, and are attached individually to the stem (versus the bundles in pine). The underside of each needle appears white due to the two bands of stomata (pores used for gas exchange). Balsam fir needles feel flat and soft to the touch; spruce needles are sharply pointed and rounder. The foliage is strongly aromatic, which contributes to the popularity of balsam fir for holiday trees and wreaths. As a gymnosperm, balsam fir produces seeds but not flowers or fruits. Pollen cones and seed cones are produced on the same tree (monoecious). Seed cones are upright and fleshy. After the winged seeds are dispersed, the seed cones often disintegrate in place. Deer and moose often consume the foliage and twigs in the winter when little else is available. Red squirrels eat the fir seeds and cones. The Penobscot Nation of northern New England and Canada, along with the Iroquois Confederacy of upstate New York and Canada, used the sap of balsam fir on cuts, sores, and burns. The sap protects the tree from infection, and research has found it has antibacterial properties and is effective against common bacteria, like *Staphylococcus aureus*, that can cause illness in humans.

— *Chase Twichell*

Poisoned Arrow

A heron in wetland, unmoving.
No, not that pure. Closer to a crow

sidestepping his way along a balsam branch,
checking out the feeder below.

Still closer to the ravenous
starlings that drive away

all the other birds.
First love, that poisoned arrow.

HABITAT AND RANGE: Black birch is common in forests and along stream banks and can be an early successional tree in disturbed areas. It can tolerate variable soil types and sunny to shady habitats. Range extends from southernmost Canada throughout the northeast (where it is most abundant), west to Ohio, and down the Appalachians into northern Alabama and Georgia.

DESCRIPTION AND NOTES: Black birch, like maple, is a common deciduous tree in eastern temperate forests. Trees can reach eighty feet in height but are typically shorter. Bark is gray to reddish brown and quite smooth when young. Irregular vertical cracks are common in the bark as the tree ages, but it does not exfoliate like many other birches. Birches, including black birch, have horizontal lenticels in the bark; these areas allow for the plant to exchange oxygen and carbon dioxide with the atmosphere. Pinnately veined leaves have multiple parallel secondary veins terminating at the toothed margin. Leaves have two orders of fine, irregular teeth. Leaf bases are rounded to slightly cordate (heart shaped). Black birch foliage turns a bright golden yellow in the fall. Separate male and female catkin flowers are visible around the same time the leaves appear in spring. One way to distinguish black birch from similar looking species (e.g., black cherry) is to crush the leaves or young twigs; black birch has a strong aroma of wintergreen. This characteristic threatened black birch's survival in the past as it was overharvested to distill wintergreen oil. Black birch is also susceptible to a fungal canker caused by *Neonectria gallingena*. The Iroquois Native Americans enjoyed a beverage made from steeped black birch twigs. In addition, a tonic made from black birch bark was consumed by members of the Mohegan Nation.

— *L. Renée*

Self-Portrait as the Tree of Knowing

They say I was born by the river
long-limbed and sure-

rooted—a Black birch birthed
to soil   soiled

with acid. They call me lush
with resilience,

say I reclaimed what had eroded—
shorelines   coal mines,

environments meant
to swallow me whole

with water or dirt and leave
no bark behind.   They say

they made new discoveries
by my riverside, where waterfowl

nest and wild turkey feed
on my seeds   full-bellied,

where twigs mint the mouth
with wintergreen delight.

Here, I want to say
no strange fruit.   Here,

Black means abundance, not
death. Here, I don't hear

the girl seated in the second row
of the yellow school bus, her pale

cheeks flush with spotty apples,
her throat   a rotten trunk,

turn backward, toward me,
as if winding a clock,   and lob

strange language I don't,
at first, understand—replace   *birch*

with   *bitch*—but keep the Black.
I try to hold onto my birth

story, remember they say
I was planted firm in loam, cultivated

to be tolerant of wind and ice,   unaffected
by any storm brewing a Devil's paradise.

But, O, the wet   hot   public shame
the name I was named   felled me

as if I had no roots,
no heart-

wood, old transporter,
which made me resistant

to decay, as if I could be
snapped like a flimsy

dead branch
before the death of winter,

a wimpy brittle exterior,
dry right to the dark meat

bark. I couldn't let
the girl see defeat

water down my brown
stung, nicked,

as if by a fingernail
or pocket blade scrape,

examining if there were
any proof of life left

in me, sliced into
stupefied silence. Left in me

was a knowing
that I would transform sap

into sweetener,
shed paper-thin

layers with age,
toughen and gray for a heavier

grain with which I would build
furniture and futures

sturdy enough
not   to fail me.

HABITAT AND RANGE: This common early successional tree can persist into mature woodlands. It prefers sun and rich moist soils but can tolerate various conditions. Its range includes much of eastern North America spanning from Nova Scotia to Florida and west to Minnesota, Kansas, and Texas. Varieties of black cherry can also be found in Central America.

DESCRIPTION AND NOTES: One way to recognize black cherry is by its almond-scented aromatic bark. Small branches appear reddish brown, but the trunk is typically darker except where cracks expose a lighter reddish-brown underbark. The alternate leaves are finely toothed and often have a wavy edge. Black cherry leaves are shiny on the upper surface and terminate in an acuminate apex. On the underside of the leaf, the midrib is often lined with a brown pubescence. The foliage is an excellent food source for giant silk moths, various butterflies, and inchworms. A member of the rose family (Rosaceae), black cherry has showy white flowers in late spring clustered in an inflorescence called a raceme. Each flower has five petals attached to a yellowish hypanthium (floral cup) that is visited by bees. Black (to red) fruits mature by late summer and are very popular with various bird and mammal species. The edible fruit can be used to make jelly or to flavor wine. Economically, black cherry is in demand for its high-quality wood, which is used for cabinets, furniture, and musical instruments. Multiple Native American tribes within the Northern Appalachian region have used black cherry bark to treat coughs and colds.

— *Lee Upton*

Black Cherry

In spring the honeybees fumble between
hanging ladders of blossoms,
disappearing through a seam
until clusters of fruit swell among the notched
waterworks of leaves.
Each cherry is a glowing rose
strung to a stem and knotted.
In autumn the cherry darkens,
arterial blood to venous blood,
deepening beauty as
the black cherry reminds us:
Wherever and whenever, be generous.

Although much of the tree is poisonous,
the bark brews a syrup
to soothe a child's fevered cough.
Branches become cabinets, and
plucked, the cherry, a little sweet,
may transfigure into jelly, wine, brandy.
Songbirds and black bears
and the delicate-stepping deer
show up for a feast,
while deep inside each bruised fruit
one seed waits,
ready to set a resurrection loose.

Chestnut Oak *Quercus montana*

HABITAT AND RANGE: Chestnut oak is found in well-drained dry woods with sand, gravel, or rocky substrates. It is common in uplands including cliffs. Its range includes southern Ontario, all of the northeast United States, west to Michigan and Illinois, and south to Georgia and Mississippi. South of Virginia, chestnut oak is only found inland, away from the coast.

DESCRIPTION AND NOTES: Chestnut oak is one of many oak species in Northern Appalachia. It is tolerant of acidic soils so is often found growing with understory plants of the heath family like mountain laurel and blueberry. These trees, typically topping out at one hundred feet tall, have gray, blocky, deeply furrowed bark; fissures in the bark can be reddish. Leaves are clustered at the shoot tips and have large, rounded teeth, each of which is fed by a secondary vein. The lack of bristle tips on the teeth indicates that the chestnut oak is a member of the white oak group. The underside of the leaves is pubescent (hairy) and much lighter in color than the upper surface. The wind-pollinated unisexual flowers are inconspicuous and appear before the leaves are fully mature in the spring. Fruit is an elongated nut (often shiny) with a funnel-shaped textured cupule (also known as an acorn). The acorns are consumed by various mammals and turkeys. Chestnut oak wood has an occasional use as timber but more often is used for fuel. The common name references its similarity to the leaves of the American chestnut (*Castanea dentata*), whereas the specific epithet of the scientific name, *montana*, refers to this species' preference for mountainous terrain and ridgetops.

— *Dave Bonta*

Chestnut Oak

in gun-hungry november i run
one finger down a valley
of chestnut oak bark

crushing a spongy moth egg case
grit glinting gold
in the low-angled light

its patter not unlike
the rain of caterpillar droppings
this past June

the ground is glossy
with yellow-brown leaves
a future millimeter of soil

but due to a freak late frost
again no acorns sacerdotal
as outdoor ovens

no pale tips extending
light-averse tentacles
into the fungal underworld

though this four-trunked oak
sprouted not from an acorn
but a stump

its previous incarnation felled
i imagine for its bark
the tannery by the river

extracting every last
bitter drop of yellow
to soften and toughen rawhide

the timber would've gone
into some catacomb of coal
behind the allegheny front

these four successor trunks are almost
a forest of their own
a one-tree woods

merging slowly
from the ground up
around a growing hollow

having walled off at ground level
the hole-turned-howl
where a fifth trunk had been

i think of a chestnut oak i found
the day before on the other
rockier ridgetop

with a place at breast height
where ridges in the bark converge
half-face half-fist

how marvelous i thought
a natural flourish as suggestive
as a work of art

and i circled the trunk and saw
that it was hollow
from an old lightning strike

the char still visible
through the last small
hole to heal

living in the hollow
between these two
ridgetop oaks

let me too hold the darkness close
whatever weather our shining
cities may unleash

HABITAT AND RANGE: Hobblebush is found in damp, cool, shady woods. It is more common at mid to high elevations. Its range includes the eastern portions of southern Canada, the northeast United States, west to Ohio, and south to northern Georgia. Hobblebush is more abundant in the northern part of its range and is limited to higher elevations. It is often found mixed with conifers in the southern portion of its range.

DESCRIPTION AND NOTES: Hobblebush is a broad perennial shrub up to ten feet tall. The branches often bend toward the ground and take root. When they do, they pose a substantial trip risk for a distracted hiker, hence the common name. The large simple toothed leaves are oppositely arranged. Leaves are ovate and somewhat heart shaped. Flowers are white and clustered in inflorescences that appear in the spring. The outer flowers are large and showy, likely functioning to attract pollinators, despite being sterile. The smaller flowers in the center of the inflorescence are fertile and rely on select species of bees, flies, and beetles for pollination. The red drupaceous fruits are arranged in clusters in the same positions as the fertile flowers. They are dispersed by birds. In some areas, over browsing by deer can threaten the hobblebush population. Recent research indicates that hobblebush survived the most recent glaciation in either the mid-Atlantic Coastal Plain or the Gulf Coastal Plain away from the coast. After the glaciers retreated, a population of hobblebush slowly spread north to its current range.

— *Sydney Lea*

Hobblebush

I've cursed the stuff all my life whenever I walk—
or try to walk—through thickets of it, forever
thinking that I can pick my way with care.
The thought is always wrong. My wife and I
prefer to call it by its folklore name, *witch-hobble.*
That *witch* is not related, I've discovered,
to sorcery but comes from an ancient term
for *pliant.* Still I've often half-believed
that I'd been paralyzed by some dark daemon,
that I'd stand unmoving, spellbound, till the snow
lifted me out of my impasse—or buried me dead.
I want to cut myself loose! an old friend said.
Ensnared in agony, she longed to die,

so she gave up food, intent on killing her aches
from chronic migraine. Her friends tried to intervene
but she said she was tired of being tied to pain.
As death impended, she spoke of splendid visions,
Rewards, perhaps, for misery. She could offer no joy
as ballast to her despair. Why bring this up?
Maybe to remember I'm luckier far.
Stuck in the brush or self-starvation? I ask you . . .
I should free myself from gloom by celebration,
not that I always do. But consider my loathing
for hobblebush: at a long cold season's end,
its early bloom can seem almost medicinal.
Or what may be the same, its heart-shaped leaves

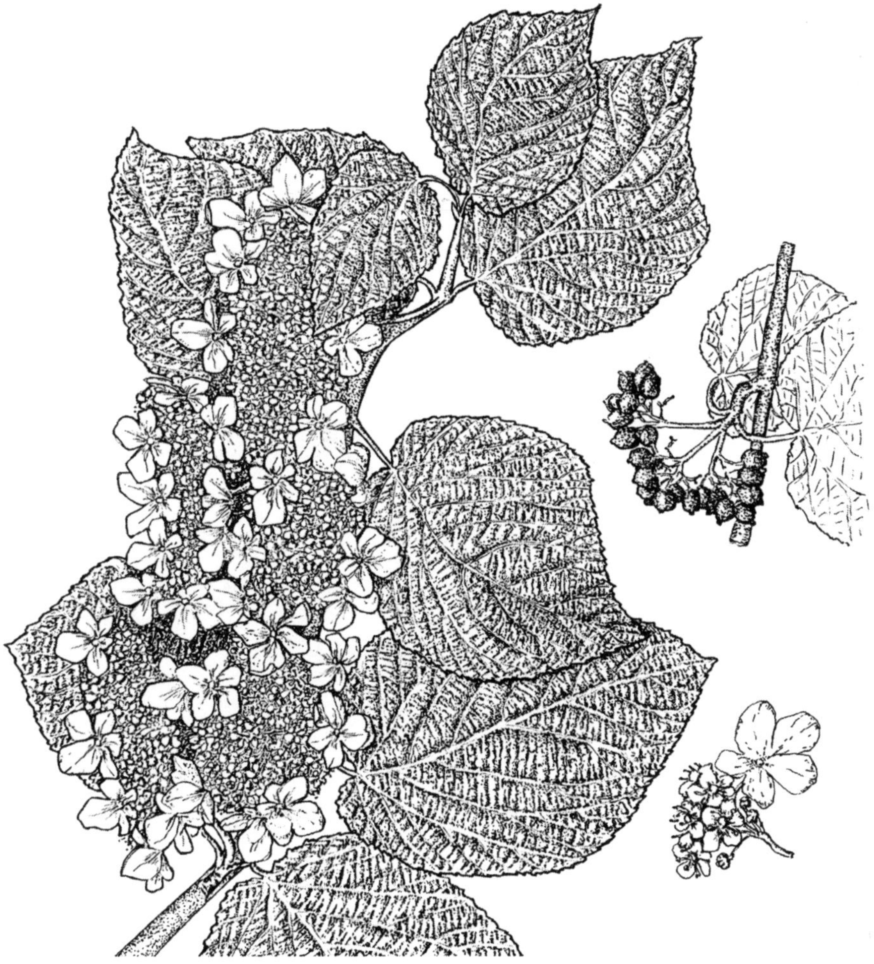

can almost seem a trope for hope. You'll note
I choose to say *almost.* I knew a man
who lived a hundred years, a Passamaquoddy.
Once we stood by a brook whose banks were bordered
as far as our eyes could see by clots of witch-hobble.
He rebuked me when I damned the shrubs out loud.
He revered their leaves for how they soothed a headache,
how elders infused the roots when the breath of life
came hard to them. I joked that *I* might use them
when my own breath turned to gasps in the hobblebush.
He didn't smile. He knew that I was groping,
that nature's not some reservoir for poets
from which they're free to cull their imagery
or their conceits. Yet I resist too rarely—

then I curse the way I'm tethered to figuration.
Why not the thing itself? Why shouldn't I watch
the whitetail deer for their sake, not my own?
They browse witch-hobble fruit in latest fall,
so the blackened berries clearly serve a purpose.
I should learn that nothing's either this or that.
The snowshoe hare, for instance, finds a haven
in hobblebush's byzantine understory
and the redtail soars away in its frustration.
Hawk and mammal: each lovely in its fashion.
I can praise witch-hobble as refuge while I marvel
at the redtail's thrilling stoop. And on the snow
a blood-script would have shown real splendors too.

Shagbark Hickory *Carya ovata*

HABITAT AND RANGE: Shagbark hickory prefers rich moist soil and ample sun. It is common in lowlands and valleys. Its range includes much of eastern North America from southernmost Canada south to Georgia and west to Minnesota, Nebraska, and Texas. A disjunct population is also present in Mexico.

DESCRIPTION AND NOTES: Shagbark hickory is a deciduous tree with mature specimens growing fifty to one hundred or more feet tall. The grayish bark peels off in large, irregular, vertical strips that often litter the surrounding ground. Young twigs and stems are hairy (and look somewhat fuzzy). Shagbark hickory leaves are pinnately compound with five (rarely seven) leaflets. The terminal leaflet is typically the largest with the basal two leaflets noticeably smaller. Leaflets have a finely toothed margin and leaves turn a golden yellow in the fall. Shagbark hickory blooms in the spring, but you are more likely to notice the large nuts with a thick husk that splits open along four seams. The edible nuts are an important food source for wildlife, and crushed, boiled nuts were used as a baby food by members of the Iroquois Confederacy. Shagbark hickory wood is valued for its strength and hardness and is used for flooring, tool handles, and baseball bats. The burning wood is also used to smoke game meat.

— *Daniel Lassell*

Frame inside a Frame

Like a resurrected god's body
offered to perplexed disciples,

the shagbark hickory
shares a hundred doorways

into itself, drooping open
to carve the air.

My brothers would rip
the shards free, swordfight

with them in our backyard.
Smacked against each other,

the pieces would shatter,
brittle as bird bones.

We'd peel the hickory's
fallen nuts into grenades

then lob them beyond
our swing set. Its leaves

served as roof and bed
to our fort of sticks.

Bare wherever our hands
could reach, the hickory

must have seemed, standing
among its fellow trees,

ridiculous, or persecuted,
or sickly.

Did we thank it or ask it
for forgiveness?

We said nothing, felt
no stir of guilt.

Instead, the hickory
filched from us

as any tree does,
our outbreaths sifting

through its core,
a kept brood.

HABITAT AND RANGE: Striped maple prefers cool, moist woods. Its range includes southeastern Canada and the northeastern United States west to Michigan and Minnesota in the Great Lakes and to Ohio south of the lakes. Striped maple generally follows the higher elevation terrain into northern Georgia.

DESCRIPTION AND NOTES: Striped maple has some characteristics that differentiate it from other members of the genus, *Acer*. It is a shorter, understory tree, typically in the range of fifteen to twenty feet, although taller specimens can reach thirty feet. Bark, especially on younger individuals, is greenish with alternating stripes of light and dark green. The stripes are less prominent in the bark of older trees and many of the green shades are replaced by white and gray. The bark is a good winter food source for mammals like deer, moose, rabbits, and beavers. Three-lobed leaves are oppositely arranged as they are in other maples. Lobes often end in an elongated, narrow point. Leaves have fine, sawlike teeth, which are smaller than the teeth of many other Northern Appalachian maple species. Leaf bases are straight across (truncate) or slightly cordate (heart shaped). The leaves of striped maple turn golden yellow in the fall. The broadly bell-shaped flowers appear in May and are larger and showier than many other maples. The five petals are yellow to greenish, and flowers are clustered in drooping inflorescences. Fruits are the two winged "helicopters" found throughout the genus. An alternate common name for this species is goosefoot maple, so named because the leaf shape is like the outline of a goose's foot. In the Northern Appalachians, striped maple is also known as moosewood because the bark is consumed by moose during the winter. The Penobscot tribe of northern New England (into Canada) used striped maple tea to treat a variety of health conditions including gonorrhea.

— *Judith Vollmer*

The Striped Maple

Unbraided,
parallel, your green-grey
stripes thick as elves' pens

climb, writing on rain and wind.
Scored on wood-rope
your music calls

to all things change-ling,
sheltered in bark-
leather thick as a child's wrist—

the better to climb—
Maybe
        verticality reaching heavenward

is a furled curtain, threaded
and sturdy, but who knows how to read
between the lines, into such heart?

White Pine *Pinus strobus*

HABITAT AND RANGE: White pine is found in dry to moist woods but prefers moist, well-drained sandy soils and ample sun. Its range includes much of eastern North America from southern Canada into Georgia. White pine can be found west to Minnesota and Iowa to northern Mississippi.

DESCRIPTION AND NOTES: White pine is the tallest conifer in eastern North America and frequently exceeds one hundred feet (prior to commercial deforestation, trees were often over two hundred feet tall). This evergreen has a straight trunk with scaly, deeply furrowed bark, which is smoother on the younger branches. Branches are nearly horizontal, but the lower ones self-prune resulting in mature trees that are often somewhat irregularly shaped. White pine has long, flexible needles that are arranged in bundles (termed fascicles) of five, making it the only conifer species in eastern North America with five needles per fascicle. Pine pollen will look like yellowish dust to the naked eye, but under magnification it has two air bladders (which look like Mickey Mouse ears) that both help disperse the pollen in the wind and orient it correctly when it lands on a female cone. The narrow, tapering seed cones are often slightly curved and lack the thorns that are present on some other species of pine. However, a collector will encounter the sticky resin present on the underside tip of each cone scale. These cone scales house two winged seeds that are dispersed by the wind. White pine was adopted as the state tree of Maine in 1945. The wood is popular and used for construction, furniture, and pulp for the paper industry. Some homeowners plant the trees on the edges of their property to create a natural privacy screen and wind break. Multiple Northern Appalachian tribes, including the Mohegan (Connecticut) and Shinnecock (Long Island, N.Y.), used white pine tea to treat coughs and colds.

— *Julie Swarstad Johnson*

Extant

Old growth upsprung
        from old growth, present tense

of white pines lengthening
        whether seedling shade

dappled or centenarian
        dappling. This tree ever

plural, less one pine
          entire than the interior

they together uphold, held air
          between them like breath

giving shape to lungs. Not
          nostalgia, this living

long in acidic soil. Not luck
          or plan alone enough to keep

their rhyme of ridge shadow
          and needle hush. More than

human arms can enfold, full
          grown and growing, years

lacing grooves through bark,
          lichen-gilt. Know them

by what they open, locus
          where we can say, outlast us.

II — Wildflowers

Allegheny Blackberry *Rubus allegheniensis*

HABITAT AND RANGE: This common bramble grows in a variety of habitats, including dry upland meadows, open woods, and along roadsides. It is found throughout the entire range of the Appalachian Mountains and beyond. It is a hardy plant and is found north to Quebec and south to Alabama and west to Oklahoma.

DESCRIPTION AND NOTES: Allegheny blackberry is a shrub that possesses multiple, thorn-covered stems. The stems or "canes" grow in an arched form and often reroot into the ground. These characteristics further classify Allegheny blackberry as a briar or bramble member of the rose family (Rosaceae). Young canes are purple, and mature canes are brown. Allegheny blackberry blooms in June through early July in the Northern Appalachian Mountains. Flowers are white, have five regular parts (petals), and provide food resources, both pollen and nectar, to native bees. These pollinated flowers develop into shiny deep-purple-black drupes by August. Wildlife including turkeys, box turtles, mice, and black bears savor these fruits. The strong, thorn-covered canes provide nesting habitat for songbirds. Blackberry fruit was an important mainstay in the diet and livelihood of Appalachian families—especially during times of economic hardship. By the end of the blackberry season, stained hands and faces identified those individuals who relied on blackberries for food or sale. Because of this association with poor, subsistence farmers of Appalachia, the nickname "briar" or "briar hopper" is used synonymously with "hillbilly" in the mountains of Ohio.

— *Julia Spicher Kasdorf*

Blackberries

On abandoned land hazy with timothy,
sweet grass, multiflora rose, black garter
snakes drape from holes in the shale bank.

Glassy beaded pips grow as purple-black
as iron ore pellets that scatter along
the railroad tracks, hot and sweet.

Whine of wasps and bees, faint thuds in
buckets, a quarter for each quart you pick,
purple lipped, feet sweating in rain boots.

Jaggers catch your arms and legs, thorns
that wove our Savior's crown, jaggers
Lucifer spat on brambles when he fell.

No wonder these berries mend ulcers, heal
gums: underground their roots run astringent.

Bluebead Lily *Clintonia borealis*

HABITAT AND RANGE: Bluebead lily is found in shady, moist woods, often at high elevations. It is most common in northern areas of the eastern United States into southern Canada. Its range extends west to Illinois and Wisconsin and south to northern Georgia, generally following the Appalachian Mountains south of Virginia.

DESCRIPTION AND NOTES: Bluebead lily is an herbaceous perennial of the forest understory that spreads via rhizomes (underground, horizontal stems). It is a monocot like grasses, orchids, and palms. Two to five (often three) elliptic smooth-margined leaves are arrayed from the base of the plant. The leaves have parallel veins running from base to apex, a common feature of monocotyledonous plants. Look for the yellowish flowers in May and June. Multiple bell-shaped flowers appear on a tall slender, stalk. Most monocots have flower parts in multiples of three and bluebead lily is no exception with six tepals and six stamens. Bluebead lily can self-pollinate, but cross-pollinated plants—pollen carried by bumblebees—have a higher rate of fruit production. As the common name suggests, the berry fruit is a brilliant shade of blue that ripens in September. Iroquois Native Americans used bluebead lily to treat both diabetes and heart conditions.

— *Abby Minor*

Learning in Low Pressure

In low pressure light
of solitude in lilyspring

weightless learning
very young that if you bloomed
later, you'd get nothing

you'd miss the boat
of light that rolls across the leafless trees

So everything untuck, up
out, ovaries & pollen

you are not a wounded dot
dangling in waves of self-

doubt, no! You are many dots of rain
you contain—dovish multitudes—

and by the deep shade comes
it comes as a sounding line in tidal green

Rolling over by cornlily
light from green to white to porcelain blue,

that's you—where—
there—ephemeral, millennial,
how long you've been the same

monocot in costume beads
in the middle of the universe
in solitude of lilyverse
at the bottom of the trees

Blue-stemmed Goldenrod *Solidago caesia*

HABITAT AND RANGE: Blue-stemmed goldenrod is common in sunny to partly shady rich woods of the eastern United States and southernmost Canada. Its range extends west to Wisconsin and eastern Texas. It is most abundant in the Northeast.

DESCRIPTION AND NOTES: There are dozens of species of goldenrod in Northern Appalachia, and many can be challenging to differentiate. The goldenrods are herbaceous perennials. Nearly all, including the blue-stemmed goldenrod, have yellow flowers that bloom from mid- to late summer through the fall. They are insect pollinated so they are not to blame for any fall allergies; ragweed—a closely related wind-pollinated plant that produces copious amounts of pollen that blooms around the same time as goldenrod is likely the culprit. Blue-stemmed goldenrod, also known as wreath goldenrod, was given its scientific name by Carolus Linnaeus in 1753. One way to identify this species of goldenrod is, of course, the stem, which is often bluish or purplish in color, smooth, waxy (can look whitish), and often arching. The one- to three-foot-tall plants have narrow leaves with serrate margins, and a pointed apex that attaches directly to the stem (sessile). The small yellow flower heads of blue-stemmed goldenrod are clustered in groups where the leaves meet the stem. Do not be surprised if you see native bees and butterflies fluttering around the blue-stemmed goldenrod as they are an important nectar source.

— *Philip Terman*

Goldenrod Hearts

Like sunrise
on the far side of the pond,
their spikey blossoms
break the heart, color

of the necessary school bus
that too soon will pause and slide
its heavy door at the corner
of Mill and Scrubgrass Road
and close. Bella and I tossed the football
as we waited, the wildflower
a wet yellow in the blinding sun
as it rose inside us.

Did we arrive here only to depart?
All parts of the plant are safe to touch.

Not to be confused
with the inconspicuous ragweed,
its bright gold filled with nectar:

Golden: to remind us of what's left
of summer; *rod*: for Aaron,
and who cast it down and it
become a snake that swallowed
the magicians' snakes, and so
it put forth buds,
and produced blossoms.

You place a vase-full beside me,
offering a little
of the summer's farewell into the house.

Wildflower of good fortune, wildflower
of pioneering spirit, wildflower signaling,
each year, for us to capture

what's left of paradise while we can.

HABITAT AND RANGE: Jewelweed prefers moist soil and shade. It is often found growing along streams or the shaded forest edge. Jewelweed is widespread in the United States, excluding the Southwest. It is most abundant in the eastern United States, and its range extends into Canada.

DESCRIPTION AND NOTES: Jewelweed is an herbaceous annual that is easy to recognize, especially when flowering. The flowers have strong bilateral symmetry (as do orchids), fused (connate) petals, and a curved spur opposite the flower opening. The flowers are on individual arching pedicels (flower stalks), that some describe as cornucopia-like. In addition to the distinctive shape, the flowers are typically bright orange in color, often with reddish brown irregularly shaped spots and patterns. The flowers frequently are pollinated by birds, but various insects can also act as pollinators. The other common name of jewelweed is "touch-me-not," which refers to its fleshy fruit capsule. When mature, it breaks open to explosively disperse the seeds, some of which become tasty treats for mice. A simple touch by a passerby can also trigger the fruit capsule to rapidly open as each valve of the capsule rolls inward and exposes the seeds. Jewelweed stems are jointed but lack hairs and are somewhat succulent, which makes them smooth to the touch. Leaves of jewelweed have long petioles and rounded teeth. A similar looking plant with pale yellow to cream-colored flowers is the related species of *Impatiens pallida*. Various Native American tribes have used the sap of jewelweed to treat poison ivy rashes, and recent research has confirmed its effectiveness. Northern Appalachian tribes have also used jewelweed for other purposes; for example, the Mohegan made a burn ointment from the dried flower buds.

— *David Baker*

Jewelweed,

touch-me-not, or in the taxonomic
registry *impatiens capensis*, can

be orange or spotted. Can be *pallida,*
in its yellow slightly larger version—

~

You're kidding. Nope. Dunk two leaves in the creek,
where it runs down cold, and you get emeralds

in your palm. I mean it. Rub the sap
where the ivy bit you—and you won't itch—

~

The flowers have tubal "elongations."
Nectar "spurs." Bumblebees love them. Ruby-

throats love them. Pollination's "very high,"
says the book. What accounts for such a name?—

~

There's two or three in the scrub-line along
the fencerow, right there, next to the ivy.

Looks like the inner ear bones of a wolf.
Like you've seen *those*. Well, pictures. It's close—

~

Don't touch that. I mean it. It's called
poison for a reason. When I was a kid

I helped my dad clear this field. I breathed in
smoke from our big brush fire, and ended up—

~

in the ICU. Like you've seen wolf bones.
It's called a doctrine of signatures.

What a thing looks like should give you its name.
Where a thing grows, its other will be nigh—

~

Come on, that's too much, who says nigh.
Get back. I'm looking to see if it smells.

There's a couple more leaning there—"poppers"—
the way the little seeds bust out. Whistle-weed—

~

Toothwort. Eyebright. Little orange balsam.
Galen said things will grow beside the thing

they remedy, waiting right there for you.
They tell you what they are. Galen's the wolf?—

—

I don't know why I come out here with you.
Sure you do. Listen, there's a whippoorwill.

That's a lonesome sound. Well, there's two of them.
You think it's going to rain? Smells like rain—

HABITAT AND RANGE: Mayapple is found in damp woods or meadows with rich, humus soil. Large patches are common throughout the eastern United States south to northern Florida and west to eastern Texas. It is also found in the eastern portions of southern Canada.

DESCRIPTION AND NOTES: This hairless perennial herb, often hitting about midcalf, can be a clue that spring has arrived. The large umbrella-like (peltate) leaves stand out on the forest floor. They have five to eight deeply incised lobes that are often partially bifurcated. You may find many individuals of mayapple clustered together as they often form dense mats that spread by underground rhizomes (horizontal stems). Nonflowering individuals will have a single leaf, whereas flowering individuals will have two leaves. Look for the nodding, solitary white flowers on a short stem originating from the split between the two leaves. The center of the one-inch or larger diameter flower will have yellowish stamens and carpels. Fruits are yellow berries with many seeds that are often dispersed by the eastern box turtle. The ripe fruit is edible, but caution is required as the unripe fruit and the rest of the plant is toxic. The active compound in the plant, podophyllotoxin, has been used to treat cancer and warts. Use of podophyllotoxin or compounds derived from it are actively being studied for their antitumor properties. Both the Delaware and Iroquois Native American tribes used the roots to make a laxative. The Iroquois also took advantage of the ripe fruits to make small cakes or dried them for later consumption.

— *Grant Clauser*

Mayapple

Like memory, even landscapes
are unreliable. One day this hollow
between two ridges reveals nothing
but frost and the snakish bloodroot
groveling between fresh breaks
in the forest mulch. Today a sea
of mayapple tumbles like river
rapids into Six Penny Creek.
It was narrow once, fast flowing
until winter opened something
upstream that water reclaimed.
In his last year my grandfather

showed me the mayapple's
granny green bulbs hidden
in the plant's parasoling canopy,
a faerie's forest only ten inches
off the ground. The whole
tumble of them connected
by rhizome trailways, roots
joining each to each, a family
sharing what it can before
all is lost to the next season,
building something that could
last the weather.

New England Aster *Symphyotrichum novae-angliae*

HABITAT AND RANGE: New England aster is common in moist, open areas including roadsides and fields. It is widespread but most abundant in the Northeast and Midwest, including the southern Great Lakes area.

DESCRIPTION AND NOTES: A member of the Asteraceae or sunflower family, this herbaceous perennial likes full sun. Flowers in this family are aggregated into dense heads and New England aster is no exception. What looks like a single flower with purple petals (that can vary from white to lavender) is actually composed of dozens of individual flowers. Those around the edge that form the "petals" are bilaterally symmetrical (termed ray flowers), whereas the flowers in the center are radially symmetrical (termed disk flowers). The showiness of New England aster flowers is also due to its golden yellow disk flowers, a contrast to its purple ray flowers. New England asters typically have numerous blooms that appear from late summer to early fall and often attract butterflies. Fertilized flowers are replaced by hairy achenes (a dry fruit) at the end of the growing season. Plants can grow up to six feet tall—something to keep in mind if you are adding them to your garden for native color. Both the stems and narrow leaves that clasp the stem are hairy. The leaves often have stiffer hairs on the upper surface and softer hairs on the lower surface. Iroquois Native Americans were known to use the New England aster both to treat fever and as an aphrodisiac.

— *Kerrin McCadden*

Asters

Nights are longer now
in the north, the sun lower,
the sky a great eyelid.
Summer treads water farther
and farther out. It's cold
at night, and I like it, my knees
surprised. Halfway between
peak and nadir—I put my toes
away for another year,
and the roadsides fill with asters
like defiant children
who won't put on their coats.

Last gasp of flowers, coming up
along roadsides and old fields,
hardscrabble and thrifty,
all the bees and monarchs
to themselves, everyone gathering
firewood while they hold out,
garish and lovely, these tiny royalties
say what I keep trying to know,
that this late part of life
among the scuff and countdown
is worth an upturned face.

HABITAT AND RANGE: Teaberry is found in dry to moist woods, including on acidic soils, throughout much of the eastern United States and into southern Canada. Its range extends west to Minnesota and Illinois and south generally following a broad swath of the Appalachian Mountains into northern Georgia.

DESCRIPTION AND NOTES: Teaberry, also known as American wintergreen, is a low-growing (typically under six inches tall) evergreen plant with reddish stems. The pinnately veined leaves can be various shapes but taper to a short petiole that attaches to the rest of the plant. The white, pendulous, urn-shaped flowers are replaced by bright red berries after fertilization that can persist into the winter. The foliage, colored stems, and berries provide a pop of color against a forest floor of brown fallen leaves shed by neighboring deciduous trees in colder months. The leaves and berries are a beneficial food source for animals, including small mammals, when little else is available. Teaberry smells like wintergreen and was historically a source of wintergreen oil used in toothpaste or candy. It is often found on acidic soils with other members of the heath family (Ericaceae), including mountain laurel or rhododendron. Teaberry has an extensive history of use by Native American tribes in the Northern Appalachian region. Many tribes used it to treat kidney issues. The Iroquois also used the fruits in various food items including small cakes.

— *Robin Becker*

Teaberry

A creeping stem, a waxy leaf
in dappled light the scarlet berries feed

the waxwing pausing in the snow
a red bulb in her mouth   The leaves

when crushed will scent the air
with Wintergreen, will make a tea

that tastes like Clark's Teaberry Gum
of Pittsburgh (you can see the ad

on YouTube, learn the little dance)
Along stream banks, in clay or loam

the dense white flowers rise in spring
Adapted to retain all that

it needs, Teaberry answers
to Boxberry and Checkerberry

in Pennsylvania hardwoods where
spicy fruit sustains the fox and grouse

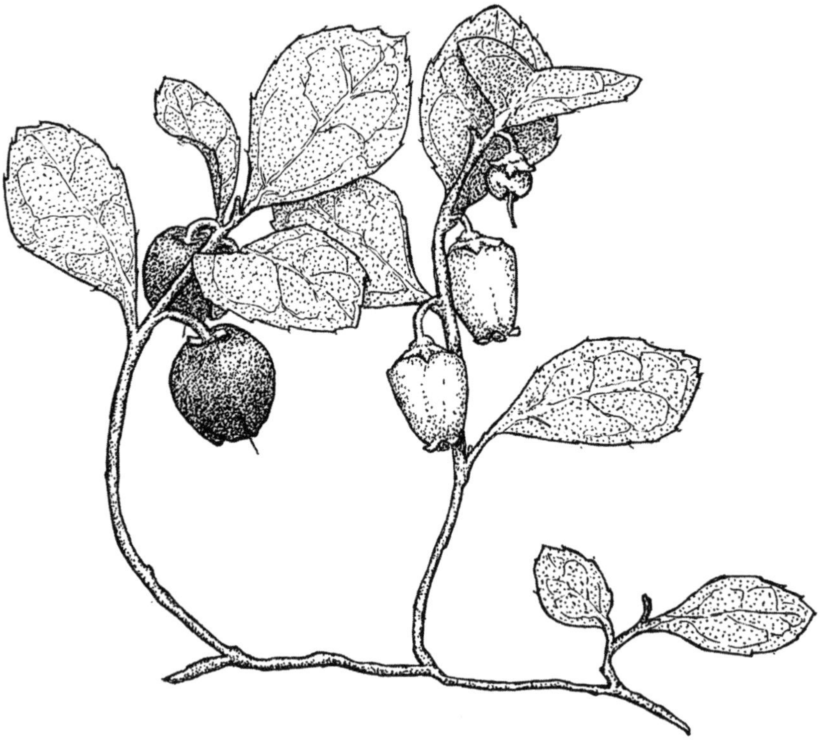

Wood Sorrel *Oxalis montana*

HABITAT AND RANGE: Wood sorrel is found in rich, moist woods in shady or cool locations. It prefers rich, humus, acidic soil and is common at high elevations or near swamps or bogs. Its range includes the eastern United States (excluding Florida) into southern Canada. It is found west to Minnesota and Indiana; south of Pennsylvania, most occurrences follow the Appalachian Mountains.

DESCRIPTION AND NOTES: The herbaceous perennial wood sorrel can be a welcome treat to find in shady, moist, wooded locations. Wood sorrel is palmately compound, and each leaf is divided into three heart-shaped leaflets. Leaves all originate from the base of the plant and are arrayed on long petioles. White five-petaled flowers arise from individual stalks; look for the pink and yellow accents on the petals. Wood sorrel flowers appear from May through the summer months. If you were out for a moonlight walk, you are likely to see wood sorrel in its "sleeping" position. Wood sorrel responds to changes in light levels by folding down its leaves. This movement is accomplished by turgor or water pressure changes in the pulvini, the swellings at the base of the leaflets. Wood sorrel is edible in small quantities, but large portions are dangerous due to the presence of oxalic acid. Oxalic acid was so named because it was first extracted from a related *Oxalis* species in the 1700s.

— *Charity Gingerich*

Homesteading the Body

Imagine, if we, in the post-Eden paradise of industrial dailyness,
got to rebuild our bodies like homesteads on the frontier.

We would become foragers again, attune to woods and wind
and the ways the pieces of us—hearts, bones and blood—

are mirrored back in nature. I am taking a course on harmony/
disharmony, otherwise known as aging,

here in the waiting room that is pre-menopause,
where out-of-date magazines are little comfort,

and the doctor is never in. My teacher is a rural healer
who tells me the plants we should eat/drink mimic

parts of the body needing attention: cut a carrot
down the center and at the end you will find a hidden eye;

red beets are high in nitric oxide which is good for the heart;
horsetail grass looks like a waving skeleton and is high in silicon,

which is what our bones need. So wood sorrel,
with its *fragile, heart-shaped leaflets,* must be

for invisible diseases of the heart: hard-heartedness,
broken-heartedness, double heartedness.

An herbaceous weed with many names:
oxalis, shamrock, toad sorrel, sourgrass, sour trefoil,

there is nothing particularly special about it,
just as there is nothing special about a heart

deceitful above all else; except there is. From decoctions
to an essential ingredient in cancer-healing tea to

St. Patrick's object lesson of the doctrine of the trinity,
wood sorrel, with its pinecone-shaped creeping rootstock

and the improbable mimicry of its tripartite
leaves that *fold in half at night, or in dry soil, or heavy rain,*

is a microcosm of history of the heathen heart. A tiny reminder
that disharmony leads us to our work. We the civilized sick,

in our temples of either/or, prone to lionize inventors
of machines and curse herbalists as witches, live out

what Ecclesiastes calls violent vexation and vanity; woe,
vow, portion, power that crushes the heart in every form—

burl, conch shell, nest—until we no longer remember any Sabbath rest,
healing. Imagine every ruin is a new frontier. Imagine

the fist of your heart as you eat a salad of violets,
dandelion leaves and sorrel greens come spring, and call it grace.

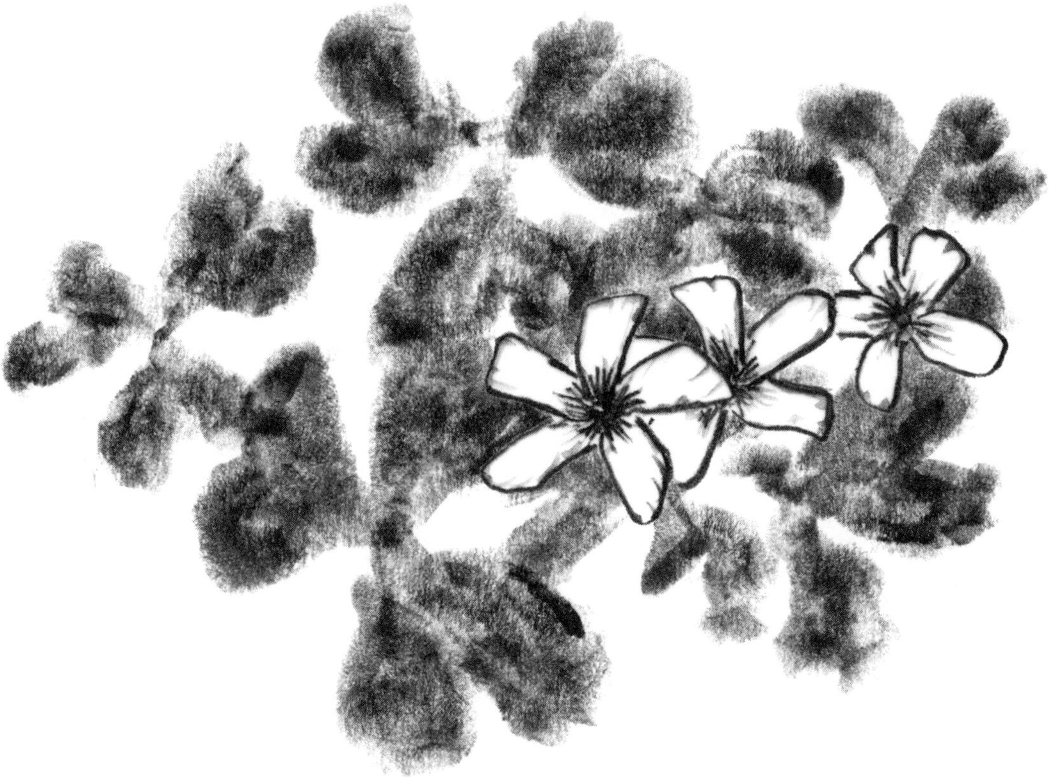

III — Mammals

HABITAT AND RANGE: Found throughout Canada and North America as far south as northern Mexico, beavers are only absent from the southwestern deserts. Once extirpated from much of this range due to fur harvesting, beavers have recovered and occupy and create wetland swamps along rivers and streams.

DESCRIPTION AND NOTES: The beaver is an aquatic rodent that is an engineer of the landscape of North America. Beavers create large mud and twig dams along moving water that form still swamps and flooded forests. These rich wetlands, in turn, create habitat for waterfowl, aquatic plants, and standing dead timber that house cavity-nesting birds. Beavers are the largest rodent in North America and can weigh up to one hundred pounds. Beavers have a thick, water-resistant, dark brown coat that was a valuable commodity sought by early European settlers and fur trappers. Beaver distribution, therefore, dictated early European exploration and settlement patterns in the Appalachian Mountains. Due to overharvesting, beavers were extirpated from most of Appalachia by 1750. Today, beavers are making a comeback throughout their former range, and you may see the sign of their handiwork along Appalachian waterways. These signs include chiseled tree trunks, lodges made of branches, and conspicuous mud and wooden dams. Primarily nocturnal, you may see beavers swimming at dawn and dusk with twigs in their mouths as they busily work to build, expand, and repair their dams. Beavers are herbivores and eat bark, twigs, leaves, and aquatic plants. Living in family groups, females give birth to three to four kits in their lodges in early spring. Beavers are susceptible to overharvesting because females are not capable of giving birth until age two or three—quite old for a rodent. Beavers signal danger by slapping their broad, flattened tails on the water surface prior to diving underwater. Native American legend relates that the beaver got this flattened tail when a large tree fell on it. The beaver was disappointed that its beautiful tail had been crushed, but the Creator explained that this new tail would help him swim rapidly and permit him to send messages to his friends.

— *Talley V. Kayser*

Suppose Your Mother Is a Beaver

after Pattiann Rogers

Suppose, before your birth, your mother fed
on cached willow she carefully anchored
into the pond-bottom during the autumn
because she knew with her body
the word "winter."

Suppose, before your birth, each night
meant labor to your mother. Suppose your mother
stirs to work in every dark. Suppose her: muscled
and unafraid, nonchalant with power.
Your mother fells one birch. She fells another,
her body sure of the direction each will fall.

Your mother's hair is rich and guarded. Her teeth
are iron eloquence. Your mother fells one aspen,
then another. Digs canals, hauls wood to water.
Her skilled hands lay limb on limb, then stone, then limb.
Her hands work, always, alongside your father's.

They fell and heave and plait, together.
They build. They build. Their work is never
settled, even as wide water gathers—
even as, in depth of winter,
they tandem-dive below the shelter
of a watchful shield of ice. And stay awhile.

Conceive of yourself, begun with such encounter:
a warm exchange of scents through brumal cold.

But your mother (and you) are bodied
against all cold. Your lodge steams quietly at first light.
You nuzzle and play, become a bristle-whiskered strength.
You sleek through water. You learn the chiseled power
in your mouth, learn the directions aspens fall
and which willow-thicket (this year)
to let keep growing, and even if

you never think "replenish" or "aquifer," never configure
your worth in fixed nitrogen, habitat, dollars
your body knows: each limb will stave away
the drought. And drought is coming.

Creature, the drought is coming.
Does your body know the word "build"?

Use your teeth. Use your muscle,
use your skilled hands—creature, build.

Black Bear *Ursus americanus*

HABITAT AND RANGE: Endemic to North America, black bears range from southern Alaska/Canada to northern Mexico, occupying forested areas, wetlands, farms, and suburban human landscapes. They are the most commonly and widely distributed bear in the western hemisphere.

DESCRIPTION AND NOTES: The largest omnivore that you will encounter in Northern Appalachia is the black bear. In fact, black bears reach their largest size (~six hundred pounds), greatest density (one to three bears per five square miles of forest) and have the highest reproductive rate (one to five cubs per female every two years) in the Northern Appalachians. These traits are due to the prolific availability of their preferred foods: soft and hard mast. Although black bears are proficient predators of newborn fawns and small mammals, they reach their large size by consuming huge quantities of blueberries, blackberries, beech nuts, acorns, hickories, and insects. Allegheny mound ants (*Formica exsectoides*) are a favorite food. Black bears are found in all Appalachian habitats but, despite their large size, are quite secretive and can be surprisingly quiet as they move through the landscape. Black bears enter hibernation in late fall or early winter and will delay hibernation until they gain enough weight to survive their winter sleep. Therefore, you may observe bears well into December in years with lower mast availability. Female bears give birth to their cubs while in winter dens and emerge in March–April to forage. Periods of increased foraging are called hyperphagy and are the times (late autumn and early spring) when you are most likely to see black bears. Observing a black bear marks a special, sacred encounter. Native American tribes of the Appalachians, including the Mohicans, Lenni-Lenape, and Susquehannock, revere the bear. Each tribe's cultural view of the bear varies; however, at the core, the bear represents authority, good medicine, courage, and strength.

— *Jerry Wemple*

Ursa

Sometimes one will come lumbering like a drunken ex-lineman, heavy footed, swaying a bit. They don't venture more than a block or two into town. Usually, it's early spring, weeks before the first fawns are spotted in the fields near the woods off the state road. Weeks too before those fields sprout full green, shake off the last clumps of snow. A couple years back, one was up on the hill near the hospital, tipping over garbage cans behind the college kids' rental houses, eating the

remnants of pizza boxes and clatter-rattling the empty cans of cheap beer. Someone called the police, and this guy, second year on the job, tries to run off the bear with a siren, but calls the sergeant to bring the shotgun and slugs just in case. I stood on my porch, saw the sergeant arrive, somehow use his SUV to herd the bear back over the hill, geehawing through an open window, pushing the reluctant creature past the cemetery and off into the woods. It wasn't much of a to-do. A neighbor woman had her shepherd's hook bent like modern art; a hardware store bird feeder got busted all to bits. *Ursus americanus*. The largest one ever killed in the state weighed 875 pounds, but I reckon getting that big is rare. The only time I ever saw one eye to eye was five years back. I was up at a friend's cabin for the week and went for a walk before dinner. I was a mile down the dirt road when he came out of the woods, nearly noiseless despite his size. There was likely fifty feet between us, maybe more, but it felt like less. When he noticed, he turned to face me, and then stood tall. Hard to say how tall. Fear doesn't make for accurate memories. He went back on all fours and rambled across the road into the deep woods. I could say I thought any one of a million things in the moment but that would be a lie. Here's what I say now: It was a wonder to see the sun leak through an opening in the trees and then disappear into the dark fur of his broad back, and to hear the fading trail of the deep gargle of his voice as he moved away, surely certain of his world.

Bobcat *Lynx rufus*

HABITAT AND RANGE: Ranging from southern Canada to northern Mexico, bobcats are habitat generalists and are found in wetlands, deserts, scrublands, and forests. In the Appalachians, bobcats are most commonly found in forests and wooded swamps.

DESCRIPTION AND NOTES: Bobcats are one of three native felines in the Appalachians. The others are the mountain lion (*Puma concolor*) and Canada lynx (*Lynx canadensis*), both of which were extirpated from the Appalachians due to habitat loss and overharvesting. Today, Canada lynx only are rarely encountered in northern Maine, and there are periodic, unconfirmed sightings of mountain lions. Bobcats, unlike these other cats, persisted in the Appalachians, perhaps due to their smaller size (twenty-five pounds), nocturnal habits, and generalist diet. Bobcats eat small mice, voles, squirrels, reptiles, and birds. They also tolerate human-modified landscapes and inhabit forests, farms, and suburban areas. In May, bobcats give birth to three kittens in dens that can be rock piles, caves, or hollow logs. Kittens will stay with their mother for eight to ten months learning to hunt and kill prey. Bobcats are very secretive and are rarely seen. However, you may find their tracks, and you can distinguish their footprints from other carnivores because their retractable claws are not evident in the print. Bobcats vocalize like other cats and will hiss, growl, and create loud scream-like calls during their late winter breeding season. The common name of this felid refers to its short, black-tipped, "bobbed" tail, which is due to a genetic mutation found in the *Lynx* genera of felines. Bobcats are partially the inspiration behind the Wampus cat, a mythical creature described in Appalachian folklore and Native American myths. Most commonly encountered in Southern Appalachia, Wampus cat has the face of a bobcat and, in Native American legend, is the embodiment of a watchful, half-woman, half-cat, bipedal creature that protects its people. European settlers of Appalachia viewed Wampus cat as a more sinister and dangerous monster that attacked livestock and could drive a person insane.

— *Roger Mitchell*

Just Shy of Being

> This world is not conclusion
> A species stands beyond
> —EMILY DICKINSON

The bobcat strode straight across the small field
in back of us and up onto the stone wall.

I shouted downstairs to Dorian. She
got there just as it struck a determined line

across the moss and with no fuss or fear
disappeared into the woods a neighbor owns

but never visits. Another who stays just
shy of being among us. Or, possibly, one of us.

Eastern Chipmunk *Tamias striatus*

HABITAT AND RANGE: Eastern chipmunks are found throughout the United States and Canada, west to the Mississippi River and south to northern Georgia and Alabama. They prefer deciduous forests that are dominated by mast trees (oaks, hickories) but have adapted to human landscapes, including urban parks and suburban developments.

DESCRIPTION AND NOTES: The scientific name for eastern chipmunk, *Tamias striatus*, translates to "striped housekeeper." It is a fitting name, as you will most likely encounter this ground squirrel collecting hard mast (acorns, hickories), leaves, and birdseed for storage in its "house" or burrow. Chipmunks are one of the most common squirrels in Appalachian forests, but they also make themselves at home in backyards, city parks, and other human landscapes. The chipmunk's stripes indicate that this species evolved in the dappled light of the Appalachian forest floor where the stripes provide camouflage from aerial and terrestrial predators. Tales from the Iroquois and Mohican Nations, however, claim the chipmunk's stripes are evidence of an escape from the claws of a black bear. Chipmunks are territorial, and individuals defend a fifty-foot radius area around their burrow. Territoriality only breaks down during breeding season and at concentrated food sources (e.g., birdfeeders). Eastern chipmunks are highly vocal, and researchers have deciphered the meaning behind their vocalizations. Clucking is a signal that an aerial predator has been spotted; chipping is reserved for terrestrial predators; and trilling is directed at kin to warn them of danger. A chipmunk chorus is often heard in the autumn forest, but they are silent during winter when they spend time in their burrows feeding on stored mast.

— *J. L. Conrad*

As in an Emergency

The chipmunk lies stretched in a narrow cardboard box like a specimen, cheek pouches taut over a last gathering of seeds. Her fur rumpled. A clump of dirt clinging to her teeth. The chipmunk whose momentum carried her along the footing of the house, under the Solomon's seal, an arcing, parabolic run. Dried grass cups her inert body. Whose trajectory came to an end in the teeth of the juvenile schnauzer mix chasing a tennis ball and returning instead with a mouthful of fur and bone and its heart the size of a human fingernail. The chipmunk's belly rises and falls. Her four-fingered front paws tucked against her chest, her tail's fine brushwork lifting in the October air before coming to rest. Yet in my dream, the improbable occurs: the chipmunk stirs back to life, curling her body into the comma of sleep, her heart pulsing just four times per minute. In winter, on sunny days when the air stills, hushed and breathless, the chipmunk will wake and eat the stores she has set aside for exactly this time.

HABITAT AND RANGE: Fishers are widely distributed in forests across the northern United States and Canada. Endemic to North America, fishers prefer mixed coniferous-deciduous forests and have been reintroduced to areas (e.g., Pennsylvania) where they were previously extirpated.

DESCRIPTION AND NOTES: The largest member of the weasel family in the Appalachians, the fisher has recently returned to portions of its former range after decades of extirpation. Due to overharvesting, habitat loss, and declines in prey resources, fishers were extirpated from portions of Connecticut, Pennsylvania, and New Jersey. Reintroduction efforts and natural expansion has resulted in fishers' presence in the forests of Northern Appalachia today. The fisher, also called the "fisher-cat," readily climbs trees where it efficiently hunts birds, squirrels, and porcupines—a specialty. The fisher, however, does not eat fish, and its common name derives from the European word for ferrets (polecat)—*fitchet*. Their lush coat is a deep chocolate brown; they have a long, bushy tail and can reach three feet in length. These traits give fishers an almost shadowlike quality as they move through the forests. Fishers are solitary, secretive hunters, so they are rarely seen. However, you may see fisher tracks in the snow. Fishers, like all weasels, have a bounding gait whereby they move their front and hind feet in tandem resulting in a side-by-side footprint pattern. In Native American folklore, fishers are portrayed as heroic and brave, and an Algonquin tale describes the Big Dipper constellation as a fisher. The story explains the presence of the fisher in the night sky, describing how other animals tried to reach the North Star but froze to death in their efforts. The fisher was able to get closest to the North Star, but he only continues to revolve around it—representing the way constellations rotate around Polaris.

— *John Hodgen*

The Fisher

Back away, slowly, a field guide (or urban legend) might say.
The Fisher will take your hand. The Fisher will take your arm.
And that scream, so like the baby left in the boreal woods
by the huntsman who would not kill Snow White, the reason,
perhaps, Thornton Burgess never told The Fisher's story to anyone
in his House of Burgesses, though he urged us to step freely toward
Peter Rabbit or Mr. Mocker, to whom The Fisher clearly owes a debt,
that voice, that shared screen, in the deepest part of the night.

Perhaps that baby's cry, that *Scream* of Munch's is all we know
or can divine. A hiss all it is, the rest debunked, conspiracy theory,
the scream not his but his victims': baby fox or even porcupine.
We enter this world crying, and go out the same, rabid with tears
and wailing at the light and its loss. The rest is all work and wonder,
the little deaths along the way, The Fisher our guide, our forester,
calling out to wake us again and again. And are we not called,
as Jesus said to Peter, to become fishers of men?

Mink *Neovison vison*

HABITAT AND RANGE: Mink inhabit forested areas along streams, rivers, ponds, and lakes. The best habitat for mink includes rocky areas with some shrub cover along waterways. Mink are found throughout Canada and the United States—only absent from Arizona and Hawai'i.

DESCRIPTION AND NOTES: Mink possess a rich, chocolate brown coat and a white chin patch but appear black from a distance. Like all weasels, mink have a slender body and short legs. Mink are eighteen to twenty-four inches long with a slightly bushy tail and, if seen at night, will have a yellowish green eyeshine. Primarily nocturnal predators, mink capture and eat crayfish, fish, frogs, shellfish, small mammals, birds, and larger prey like muskrats and rabbits. An excellent swimmer, this semiaquatic mammal has partially webbed feet and hunts as effectively in the water as on land. The fur trade brought the first European explorers to the Northern Appalachians, and wild mink populations declined sharply in the 1800s due to widespread trapping. Since captive farming of mink began in the mid-1900s, wild mink populations have rebounded, and they are frequently seen foraging along the rocky banks of streams in the Appalachian Mountains. Mink release musk from an anal glad to mark their hunting territory—a characteristic of all Mustelids. The resulting strong smell is reflected in the Cherokee word for mink—*svgi*, which is the same word used for the onion plant. Mink rely on clear, clean, cool water that supports abundant prey and are, therefore, good indicators of environmental quality. During the global coronavirus pandemic, mink were found to be as susceptible to the disease as humans and were the first species found infected in the wild.

— *Leah Poole Osowski*

Mink

The river forgets its name.

Ice riven by the current   the pull of memories
                    unremembered
and the mink are not innocent.

Their violence accepted   how brisk.

New moon eyes and a mouth straight
for the neck of the swan.

No sky, no opulence, no collars up against the windchill.

The mink twist their bodies inside their skin.
This is one mechanism.
                                        Helter skelter   discreet you.

Owned silence ever in motion   defined territory
riverbank torn in its allegiances.

Twilight turned off
                      they slow their hearts in the cool water.

The white patch under their lip is just a rumor, as in,
they did not love you, as if
                                        the fish could survive the attack,
                                        albeit vicious, vicious.

Their bodies are canals.   Their bodies are a calling.

I'd follow them to the bottom of the waters
imbibe on every ankle-height pleasure we've never endured.

HABITAT AND RANGE: In North America, moose occupy the boreal forests of Canada and the northern United States, including the Rocky Mountains and northern New York and New England. They prefer coniferous forests that contain wetlands and ponds and are also found in riparian areas dominated by willow and aspen.

DESCRIPTION AND NOTES: The scientific name for moose is derived from an ancient word—*alces*—that is similar in many Old World languages, including Scandinavian, Greek, Latin, and Irish. This etymological similarity indicates the global distribution of this largest member of the deer family. However, the common name used in North America is an Algonquian word—*moòs*. Moose were an important food animal to the Algonquian and represented endurance and survival. Moose are by far the largest mammal found in the Appalachians, with males averaging six feet tall at the shoulder and weighing 1,400 pounds. Bull moose are further distinguished by their huge, flattened antlers. Their antlers, which are shed and regrown each year, can reach five feet in width and weigh thirty pounds. Due to their dark, almost black, fur, moose can be surprisingly hard to see in the dark undergrowth of Northern Appalachian coniferous forests. You will most likely encounter moose feeding in lakes and ponds where they will submerge their head (and sometimes their entire body) to forage for aquatic plants. Be cautious when you see moose. Bulls are aggressive during the fall breeding season, and cows will boldly defend their calves, which are born in late spring. The moose is the state mammal of Maine.

— *Betsy Sholl*

The Moose

We met in the marsh,
where she and her calf munched.

I was the mooch in this scene,
brief jogger passing through.

The ranger had warned
she'd be a good kicker

if her kid was in danger,
and there I was, the other.

But I had gone too far
to turn back, so we stood—

the goofy-looking magnificent she
with stringy green mulch-like

muck dripping from her mouth
and pale, breathless jog-tired me

trying not to threaten.
We stood staring,

sharing a stand-off
for one long brief moment

till she sized me up,
then twitched her ears

and tail as if flicking off
flies and turned back

to swilling up swamp,
letting me pass—slowly

and so close I could almost,
not quite touch that dewlap

and hump, stunned
no longer wanting to run.

HABITAT AND RANGE: Porcupines in North America occupy all of Canada and are distributed as far south as northern Mexico in the west and southern Pennsylvania in the eastern United States. Porcupines are found in deciduous, coniferous, and mixed forest habitats throughout their range.

DESCRIPTION AND NOTES: The common name for this woodland rodent means "quill-pig," but the scientific name originates from the Greek and denotes an animal with an irritating back. Both names refer to their hairs that are modified to sharp spines that cover the dorsum of this distinctive mammal. Although porcupines once ranged throughout the Appalachians, they were extirpated south of Pennsylvania due to habitat loss but still inhabit the Northern Appalachian forests. Porcupines differ from other rodents not only in appearance but in several other life history traits. Unlike other rodents, porcupines have a low reproductive rate only giving birth to one "porcupette" each year. In addition, porcupines have a distinctive yearly migration pattern. They spend summers feeding on herbaceous forbs and grasses on the ground but become arboreal in winters—often spending weeks at a time in the same tree where they eat buds, bark, and twigs. Therefore, you can scan bare tree canopies in winter and look for their distinctive round, yet spikey, silhouettes. You may also find their pellet-shaped droppings mounded under a favorite tree. Despite common lore, porcupines cannot "shoot" their barb-tipped quills at predators, and quills must be removed if attached—they will not fall out on their own. Successful predators of porcupines must flip the animal on its back to access the quill-free belly. Porcupine quills were, and are, highly valued by Native American tribes who create intricate, sacred quillwork to decorate clothing and ceremonial items—the oldest form of embroidery used by Indigenous peoples.

— *Marjorie Maddox*

Field Notes: The Porcupine

He loves me.
He loves me not
comes down to piss—
foreplay the spray before
the dance of hump and prickly kiss.
Nothing shy in their raucous cries
of mate-to-mate celebrations that make
and shape a springtime porcupette—

just one small fuzzball, perfect
for preening and memes.
                                        But why
begin with this
beginning? Surely,
the hollow three-inch quills
would better thrill a listener's sharp
imagination or—contrariwise—best terrorize
by grabbing fear by rodent tails and swinging readers
round and round until they land on what they want to hear
or don't. That is, the flesh. Theirs and the unembraceable
porcupines. But here the tale both plods and thickens,

the outdoor theatre of forest or wood
ripe with pointed twists.
                                                  So let's back up
to behinds—the fashion pigs' punky backsides
and debonair spiky attires: gray-black-brown decoy hair
and highlighted tresses that camouflage pain—
the hidden and unexpected kind—
that hurt us most but still
                                        sharpen the plot
with 30,000 spines designed to—simply put—impale
our most vulnerable identities. True, joined to skin,
the microscopic barbs fan out. But who's
the predator? Who's the prey?
The warning signs are there:
pungent, musky cologne,
instinctual tail slap
for those who come
too close, the painful sting of spear
surprisingly accompanied by greasy antibiotics.
                    He loves me?
            He loves me not?
O armchair amour, why suffer slings and arrows
so unnecessarily? Labeled *slow, cute,* or *vicious,*
even rodents clothed in spikes respond only
if/when attacked. Check your Field Notes
and plan accordingly your own
happy or unhappy
  end.

Red Squirrel *Tamiasciurus hudsonicus*

HABITAT AND RANGE: The American red squirrel is found throughout Canada and the mountains of eastern and western United States. They prefer coniferous forests and rely on the seeds and cones of evergreen trees as an important food resource.

DESCRIPTION AND NOTES: Also called chickaree or boomer, names that evoke the loud chattering sounds they make, red squirrels are the smallest tree squirrel in the Appalachians. Red squirrels will most likely be heard before they are seen. This small squirrel (eleven inches long including its tail) is bold and agile and will scold other squirrels, predators, and people from an arboreal perch. Red squirrels are most closely associated with coniferous forests, and they particularly like the cones of spruce and fir, which they will collect while they are still green. Red squirrels cache these cones in middens and will feed on the stored food throughout the cold winter months. Red squirrels are territorial and defend their nesting locations and stored food supplies. They will not hesitate to chase and attack any perceived threat—regardless of size. As their name conveys, red squirrels have a deep red coat and display a black stripe along their flanks during the summer months. They are active at all times of day and temperatures, and their calls make them conspicuous in the forest canopy. Although pine seeds are favored foods, red squirrels will also eat and cache black walnuts, acorns, fungi, and hickory nuts. They remain fiercely territorial except during the breeding season in early spring and summer. Squirrel kits are born one month after the breeding season and are independent by their first autumn. Juvenile red squirrels may have to travel several miles to set up their own territories.

— *Sarah Barber*

Red Squirrel

How she can stand it
when the spruce by the road
are too new for nests
and the woodlot is all hardwood,
hemlock, downed white pine—
when even in the back field's
stand of Scotch pine dogs
nose in at the midden,
at scattershot cone scales
on an old log, at the bolt hole

in snow—when no chick-
chick-chickarees guard
her solitary larder—when
I've stomped all over everything
in my big black boots.

Snowshoe Hare *Lepus americana*

HABITAT AND RANGE: Snowshoe hares live throughout Canada and the mountain ranges of western and eastern United States. They are found in wetlands, forests, and thick, shrubby habitats—especially areas dominated by conifers.

DESCRIPTION AND NOTES: Snowshoe hares' fur is tawny brown April through September, permitting them to blend into the forest understory. However, starting in October, snowshoe hares undergo a molt—replacing their brown fur with a brilliant white coat tipped in black. Other Northern Appalachian species that undergo such a coat-color transformation are the ermine (*Mustela erminea*) and long-tailed weasel (*Mustela frenata*). The white winter coat offers excellent camouflage in the snow-covered forest understory of Appalachia, especially in areas of high elevation (> 2,500 feet) and northern latitudes. The snowshoe hare, however, derives its name from its large, wide hind feet. Like all rabbits, snowshoe hares do not have pads on their feet—instead the bottoms of their feet are covered with thick, stiff hairs. Their large feet and light body weight permit snowshoe hares to move effectively across deep snow, evading their predators, which include coyotes (*Canis latrans*), bobcats, and weasels. Snowshoe hares have other adaptations that contribute to their light weight and quick, acrobatic speed. These include a skull that has lacelike openings called fenestration and the practice of coprophagy. Coprophagy is the process of consuming feces, called cecotropes, after the "first digestion." This process permits Lagomorphs (rabbits and hares) to extract maximum nutrition from their cellulose-rich diet of grasses, forbs, and twigs without having to support a large, complex rumen (as found in deer). Snowshoe hares are North America's only true hare. Hares are distinguished from rabbits at birth because newborn hares, called leverets, are born with fur and open eyes—unlike rabbit kittens that are born blind and naked.

— *Lisa Bellamy*

Hare Hymn

When I hear yips,
          when I dread, when I stop
chewing clover; when I flinch—
          twig snapped under a paw—
when I tingle—electric, aware—
          when, for the instant,
I drop hunger,
          when I smell Death—

I leap, weightless,
        warrior of air,
buoyed by angels—
        nowness the true God—here!
Here, still here.

White-tailed Deer *Odocoileus virginianus*

HABITAT AND RANGE: White-tailed deer range from southern Canada to South America and are found in all habitats except for the United States' southwestern deserts. They can live in all habitats, including swamps, forests, farms, fields, and human-dominated landscapes.

DESCRIPTION AND NOTES: The white-tailed deer is the common, hoofed herbivore of Northern Appalachia. This beautiful, graceful, and majestic mammal not only inhabits the Appalachian Mountains, but its feeding habits shape the forest itself. White-tailed deer can consume up to twelve pounds of twigs, leaves, forbs, grasses, and acorns each day hindering healthy forest regeneration in some areas. Today, white-tailed deer densities can reach twelve to fifteen deer/square mile (or more) while historically six to eight deer/square mile roamed the forested Appalachians. Historically, carnivores such as the now-extirpated mountain lion and gray wolf hunted white-tailed deer, but now, humans are their main predator. Even though they are common, an encounter with a deer can be a highlight of a walk in the Appalachian forests. Despite their size—a mature buck can weigh two hundred pounds—white-tailed deer silently move through the forest. You may only see the flash of their white tail as they flag to warn other deer of your presence. White-tailed deer fawns are born in late May, and their brown coat is heavily spotted to camouflage them on the sun-dappled forest floor. Like all cervids, male white-tailed deer grow a new set of antlers each year, and racks of six, eight, or ten points may be sported by mature bucks. White-tailed deer were critical to the survival of early European settlers and the Native Americans that preceded them. All parts of the deer were used—their hides fashioned into clothing and moccasins; venison roasted, smoked, and dried; bones and antlers made into tools, weapons, and utensils. As a critical part of Appalachian culture, white-tailed deer are associated with power and fertility. Pennsylvania and New Hampshire have designated the white-tailed deer as their state mammal.

— *Margaret Gibson*

Glimpses

in praise of white-tailed deer

In yellow autumn
the dark slim trees are walking,
branched antlers atilt.

~

Beyond the window glass
two deer scamper upside-down
in the pond mirror.

~

Daily they come: a doe,
her fawn. Five, browsing. At dusk
an outcast, alone.

~

Hind foot directly
in the print the forefoot made—
such precision, such grace.

~

Soundless footfall . . .
whose life is not precarious?
Your life—my life, too.

~

They see "wide." It's hard
to focus looking straight-on.
I'm a blur they smell . . .

~

One beds down at noon
on a winter's wind-brake slope:
brown leaves in a heap.

~

The moon's an empty
socket in the deer's bleached skull
on my wood-plank wall.

~

No, don't be afraid.
Only Orion hunts here,
his belt a bright tilt.

~

No oak mast, or beech.
Namaste. I offer corn
beneath the winter stars.

~

Deer tracks: heart-shaped hooves
in fresh snow or frozen mud.
Each moment a birth.

~

Each moment, danger.
Deer-snort! This earth is their drum.
White-tail: run, run, run.

~

Wearing a hand-made
deer mask with branchy antlers,
I paw, and I stamp.

~

They stay put and eat.
We know you, old one . . . we don't mind
how you stomp and sing.

IV ⁓ Birds

HABITAT AND RANGE: Although it is most often associated with water, the bald eagle is well adapted to a wide range of habitats. It is not unusual to encounter eagles in open habitats away from water, such as agricultural lands, roadsides, or dumps. During the breeding season it nests close to water in huge, mature trees that can support their massive nests. Bald eagles are found in every state (except Hawai'i) and are year-round residents in the Northern Appalachian Mountains, although many individuals migrate out of the area for the winter.

DESCRIPTION AND NOTES: Our national bird, you would be hard pressed to find a bird more impressive and stunning than an adult bald eagle. Chocolate brown overall, their snow-white heads and tails and huge size make them unmistakable. It takes an eagle five years to achieve its adult plumage. Younger birds are mostly brown with a varying amount of white depending on their age. Fish make up the bulk of an eagle's diet, either captured on their own or by stealing from other species such as the osprey. They are famous for their massive nests, which they reuse and add to every year. These gigantic stick creations are placed in the largest of trees from which the breeding pair can easily survey their territory. No bird features more prominently in Native American culture, with connections to most tribes. For most Native peoples, the eagle was a formidable medicine bird with magical powers, as well as a symbol of strength and leadership. The story of the bald eagle's recovery from near extinction is one of the most successful conservation stories in the world. A combination of human-induced factors, most notably the usage of the insecticide DDT, reduced eagle populations by 1970 to around four hundred breeding pairs in the lower forty-eight states. After the banning of DDT in 1972, eagle populations have rebounded dramatically and continue to increase across their range.

— *Xiaoly Li*

Between the Sun and Moon

The sun starts to soften its rays. You come,
reclaiming a half-moon
behind your thousand-feathered wings. My eyes follow you,
lose you across branches of trees. This the first time I see you.

Beside the river, on top of the ancient pine,
you land and stay still. Eyes like blazing orbs. Just crowned
snowy head. Summer is your best time. Not like winter when that one-eyed
mother eagle died foraging in the snow while her mate brooded their eggs.

Golden light shines your dark brown feathers bronze. A statue.
A second chance. Not like that father eagle
who collapsed on the ice, his eyes drifting then closing,
after eating from a deer shot with a lead bullet.

Within an eyeblink, you're in the water, burly talons clutching a big fish,
wings gliding and slicing butterfly strokes through water.
Your nest grows by the year. I hope it lasts long. Not like the giant nest
torn by a storm that I found disassembled on the ground.

Along the edge of the river, you rise out of the crimson ripples.
Against the headwind, toward the moon,
you disappear from sight.

HABITAT AND RANGE: Closely tied to water, belted kingfishers can be found along any sizable flow or pond throughout the Northern Appalachians. Our most widespread kingfisher, it breeds from coast to coast, from Florida to Alaska. A year-round resident in the region, kingfishers will move throughout the winter in search of unfrozen waterways.

DESCRIPTION AND NOTES: The belted kingfisher is a unique and showy bird. It is larger than a jay and similar in its slate-blue plumage that contrasts with its white belly. All individuals have a blue collar, but only the females have the namesake rust-colored "belt" around the breast. A showy crest of feathers and a heavy, daggerlike bill all add to the kingfisher's striking appearance. The kingfisher often gives away its presence before being seen with its carrying, rattling call. Unique among other birds in the region, the kingfisher constructs its nest by tunneling into the soft earth along the banks of its favorite waterway. The eggs are laid in a small nesting chamber at the end of the tunnel, which can sometimes reach over ten feet in length. Its diet consists mainly of fish, which it hunts by scanning the water from a favored perch before plunge diving into the water in pursuit. The belted kingfisher is doing quite well across its range but often falls victim to fishing lines left hanging in trees along the margins of water. The scientific species name for the belted kingfisher, *alcyon*, comes from ancient Greek mythology about Alycone the daughter of the wind god, Aeolus. After her husband died in a shipwreck, Alcyone dove into the ocean in grief. The gods took pity on the couple, turning them into a pair of kingfishers that continue to dive together into the streams, rivers, and lakes of the world.

— *Kasey Jueds*

Belted Kingfisher

First hidden, then sudden
and low over river, and never
when I asked, but
maybe when I needed
most: *there,*
your sudden and plunge
and skittering call
calling me back
to myself, to the secret
interior deep as the tunnel
you excavate in sand,
in steep streambanks

that grow scarcer
each year, as rivers
are channeled
and dammed.
A *limiting factor,*
ecologists name it, when
the scarcity of one resource
can mean an entire species'
decline. *Controlled,*
people say, of a river
unwilded. In ancient
Ireland, tunnels in earth
led to a ritual
chamber, a sacred
center occasionally
illumined by sun.
Like your burrow,
carved between roots,
slender entryway
ending in the hollow
where your eggs
are laid, nestless,
on dirt. Lay me down
near the clear water
where you fish
by sight, where
you dive and shatter
your own reflection
again and again.
Lay me down
in the sound of you
calling—stutter
like a child's
wind-up toy—sound
that fills every hollow
between houses
and clouds, sound
that says there's nothing
that isn't river now.

HABITAT AND RANGE: A highly adaptable species, the black-capped chickadee can be found from the most remote forest tracts to suburban bird feeders. Their range extends down the length of the Appalachian Mountains, across the northern United States and Canada, and south into the Rocky Mountains. It is a year-round fixture across its range.

DESCRIPTION AND NOTES: Perhaps the most familiar bird in Northern Appalachian forests, the chickadee is a cheerful addition to any day. The solid black cap and throat, separated by a bright white cheek is an instantly recognizable combination of field marks. Its namesake "chick-a-dee-dee-dee" can be readily heard as small family groups call back and forth to each other as they move about. Despite its small size, the chickadee is one of our boldest birds, sometimes willing to feed from the hand of a patient observer near bird feeders. Native Americans viewed the chickadee as a symbol of honesty and guidance. This symbolism can be seen during spring and fall migration when migrating species, such as warblers, often form feeding flocks with chickadees as they follow these resident species around their territories. The chickadees know the most productive and safest areas to forage, and the transient migrants partake in this local knowledge. They are cavity nesters and will often excavate their own cavity in a rotting snag despite not being equipped with a powerful, woodpecker-like bill. Chickadee populations were hit hard by outbreaks of West Nile virus but are rebounding across their range.

— *Shara McCallum*

Ode to Chickadee

You rise and fall to the sound of your name,
echoing through woods. Your black cap,
like your black eye glinting, scintillates
in a field of white snow, across which
your body appears and disappears,
disappears and appears, hemming winter.
Long ago I sat beside a window, leaning out.
With an ornithologist's longing, I sought
to locate you—or was it myself—
in a place made less foreign
by my seeking, to recognize the arc
of your flight, a needle
dipping in and out of the air's fabric.

There, I sat waiting to know you, first
by sight, then by the sound your name
carved from my mouth, that room.
Chickadee-dee-dee, I mimicked,
singsonging back to you a lullaby.
But what need could you have
of human consolation? Even then I knew
you came for suet and seeds I arrayed,
entreating you stay
as days quickened into shadow.
Chickadee, wherever you flit—in memory,
in this present into which I ask you
once more to come—be with me a moment,
your birdsong inflecting the landscape
with all I know and all still I don't.

HABITAT AND RANGE: The breeding range of the common loon includes all of Canada and the northern edge of the United States. In the Northern Appalachians, loons will breed as far south as northern Massachusetts. Reliant on open water, breeding season requires large, forest-edge lakes in which to raise their young. Most individuals trade freshwater for saltwater in the winter and migrate out of the region to the coast. During migration the common loon may be found on any lake, pond, or riverway.

DESCRIPTION AND NOTES: Few birds are as sharply plumaged as a breeding loon. Glossy-black overall with a checkerboard of white spots sprayed across the back and wings. A white band of feathers spirals around the neck and a fearsome, daggerlike bill completes the look. The cry of the loon is perhaps the most well-known natural sound in the Appalachians. Those who have heard it are unlikely to forget. Males give a wailing-yodel call on territory, and pairs will synchronize their waving calls that echo off the water and surrounding forest. These haunting calls appear in Indigenous storytelling, and some tribes believed it was an omen of death. Unlike most birds, the loon has solid bones. This makes them more adept at diving and hunting for their prey of fish and crayfish underwater. However, the weight of their bones makes it more difficult to get airborne and necessitates loons having a "runway" of several dozen yards of water in order to gain enough momentum to take flight. The common loon is declining across the southern edge of its range, including in the Northern Appalachians. A combination of factors have led to these declines, mostly tied to human disturbances reducing water quality and fish populations in their breeding lakes.

— *Hannah Fries*

Namesake

Laugh-yodel on black water ripples out
like moonlight across the surface,

rises through woods,
hemlocks shifting their fringed skirts

as the call tumbles ghostly
through a bedroom window,

but the child in bed whispers, *Gavia immer,*
beautiful name, she thinks,

her grandparents' boat christened
for the bird with a sound like shimmer,

and *loon* like *luna,* untouchable and other-
worldly, even in daylight, that red eye,

that black & white precision, and then—
the dive, sleek slip-dip and disappear,

becomes an arrow shooting under
the canoe. Was it a good bargain,

trading hollow bones for flip turns,
the fish-flash beneath the surface?

Ask this wrestler of the liminal
who runs on water

until water runs out, until air
acquiesces and density falls

away. The child, dreamy,
pulls back from sleep's edge, resisting,

losing herself anyway in the tremolo
between lake and sky.

HABITAT AND RANGE: Often viewed as a winter or snow bird, the junco is a year-round resident in the Northern Appalachians. During the winter they can be found virtually everywhere there is brushy habitat, including as a common visitor to backyard bird feeders. During the breeding season they are a bit more difficult to locate as they prefer coniferous forests at higher elevations. Juncos have an expansive breeding range and are found throughout the Appalachians, across New England and Canada, and down through the Rockies.

DESCRIPTION AND NOTES: The dark-eyed junco is one of the most variable birds in North America with six different subspecies. The subspecies that calls the Appalachians home is primarily slate gray, with a white belly, and striking white edges to the tail that are most visible when they flush. Their song is a musical trill, likened to the sound of a ringing bell. Large flocks are encountered foraging on the ground next to dense cover where they flee with twittering calls when disturbed. Juncos often look antsy when foraging, owing to their tendency to flick their tails open and closed as they hop about. Nests are placed on the ground and carefully concealed by overhanging vegetation, logs, rocks, or other substrate. Juncos are doing extremely well across their range and are one of the most abundant birds on the continent. The species' scientific name, *hyemalis*, means winter and its genus name, *Junco*, translates to "bird of the bushes," indicating its preferred habitat.

— *Karen J. Weyant*

Why I Will Always Love the Dark-Eyed Junco

With slate-colored feathers and white bellies,
they look like November: gray sky above, fields

of snow below. Harbingers of winter, they arrive
under backyard birdfeeders to predict

an oncoming storm. Cracking seeds
and dried corn, they dance in short hops,

their brisk, clipped calls spilling out
as song, reminding me how as a child

I watched them from our kitchen window.
If you dream of juncos, my mother said,

you'll have a wonderful winter. Even now
when I catch a glimpse of their feathers

I hope they'll fly through my dreams.

HABITAT AND RANGE: The great horned owl has the distinction of exhibiting the largest year-round range of any native bird species in North America. They are found in every state (except Hawai'i), across Canada, and south into Central America. They are an adaptable species and can frequently be found close to human development. They prefer landscapes with a mosaic of forests and open spaces, with conifer stands for roosting and large trees for nesting.

DESCRIPTION AND NOTES: The great horned owl is a large owl, with mottled-brown plumage, yellow eyes, and two distinctive tufts of feathers on the head. Their calls are the classic hooting phrases that so many people associate with owls. The earliest nesters in the region, pairs can be heard setting up their territories in the middle of winter, and many nests have eggs by the end of January. Great horned owls do not build their own nest; rather they take over nests previously built by other large species, such as great blue herons, ravens, or other raptor species. Even after fledging, young birds remain in their parents' territory for months as they learn to hunt and fend for themselves. A fearsome predator, great horned owls are efficient hunters of skunks, crows, and smaller owl species. One of the best ways to find these owls is to follow the sounds of crows as they mob owls they have found on their daytime roosts. Their horned appearance, brutal hunting tendencies, and nocturnal behaviors made them feared by Native Americans. Many tribes viewed these owls as the wandering spirits of the dead or a herald of death. Owing to their ability to adapt to human development, this species is increasing in population across its range.

— *Geffrey Davis*

To the Great Horned Owl

The fatherlessness I carry wonders
why you would follow me, and then I learn

you wing all across the Americas:—
the way each miracle around us is

not the same understanding as watching
its barred but watching question glide suddenly

down from another going day. You have always
been listening nearer than I realized.

I have always headed in your direction.
Even when I left the West, placing names

of towns and woods I'd not spoken aloud
between me and the low-reaching true fir

where once you landed your tufted crown
only an impossible arm's length away—:

the hard yellow glare of your eyes briefly
fixing my breath to awe's eternity

before you ascended through the new dark.
Back then, I accepted losing your grace

as my car climbed into the Alleghenies.
Until, against the shrill cicadas' constant

singing, as lightning bugs constellated
fields like I'd never seen, the first night-sound

to grip me with the eeriness of belonging
was the deep timbre of your hoot out over

the Susquehanna waters, confirming
how I could choose to lift my belief now.

Noll

HABITAT AND RANGE: At home in forested areas across the Northern Appalachians, this woodpecker readily will come to bird feeders. The hairy woodpecker is a year-round resident across most of the United States and Canada.

DESCRIPTION AND NOTES: Identifying a hairy woodpecker can be tricky due to its similarity to the related downy woodpecker. The hairy can be separated by its larger size, both in body and bill, and has unmarked, white outer tail feathers. Hairy woodpeckers are also more common than downy woodpeckers the further north you go in the Appalachians. This species can often be located by its loud "peek" call that resonates through the forest. Woodpeckers play a vital role in their environments. As they hammer away at trees with their powerful bills in search of their insect prey, they create cavities. While woodpeckers will use their own cavities for roosting and nesting, they also provide valuable habitat for other forest species. Chickadees, titmice, small mammals, and bluebirds utilize these cavities as shelter, nesting, and storage areas as they are less adept at making their own cavities.

— *Jack Ridl*

It's a Hairy!

"No. It's a Downy. Note the wings. Listen
to its song." "I note its wings, and I am

listening to its song. And I also note its
bill. And if you look closely you will

see that it's longer than a Downy's. And
between its hammering, it pauses." "Uh,

you're right." And so it goes. Time and
again. But today on a cold November

eve, here in the heartwood of Appalachia
I spot two Hairys. Eight inches apart they

cling to the same branch, and as I stare,
they stare—at one another, then stretch

their necks and look skyward, then again
stare at one another, then again look

at what appears to be deep into the sky.
They perform this dancing under the slowly

reappearing stars. I turn, making sure our dog
is still in stay. She is. When I look back,

one has flown to a higher branch and hangs
upside down. And they still stare. Mating?

Testing each other for inexplicable trust?
Protecting home low in a tree's old trunk?

Guarding a hidden food supply? I've walked
out from relentless time into the ineffable

world where the Hairy lives in daily repetition,
its quiddity of survival. Under the light-

deflecting moon they sleep. And so do we.
Then at sunrise the Hairy wakes and begins its

singular life absent of loneliness. Our pockets
are stuffed with choices, few of which can be

certain while the Hairy hammers, ten a minute,
then its measurable pause. Its lodging is

somewhere near and until night falls again,
it sustains its pecking into the loosening

bark in its determined search for wood-
boring beetles. Low on the trunk's rings

of recorded years the Hairy circles up,
down, up, around, down daily creating

an unrealized ritual, its need to stay alive
making inseparable the sacred and profane.

Hermit Thrush *Catharus guttatus*

HABITAT AND RANGE: During the breeding season this species can be found in a variety of forest types but typically at higher elevations (> two thousand feet) in the Northern Appalachians. The majority of individuals migrate out of the region in the fall, but a few hardy individuals remain through the winter months. Hermit thrushes have a wide breeding range, comprised of multiple subspecies, that extends the length of the Appalachians, across the width of Canada, and down the Rockies into the southwestern states.

DESCRIPTION AND NOTES: Slightly smaller than the more-common robin, hermit thrushes are fawn brown above and white below. The combination of the spotted breast and the rufous tail are the best ways to identify this bird. Its habit of flicking its wings and raising its tail when agitated is a good behavioral field mark as well. Despite its drab appearance, the hermit thrush has one of the most beautiful songs in the Appalachians. Males advertise their presence with a fluting, haunting song that emanates from the forest, sometimes described phonetically as "oh, holy holy, ah, purity purity, eeh, sweetly sweetly." During the warmer months, their diet mostly consists of invertebrates. However, their ability to switch to a frugivorous diet in winter makes them unique among other insectivorous birds, allowing them to remain in the region year-round. The hermit thrush has a stable population in the region and is becoming a more common winter species aided by the presence of invasive berry species, such as oriental bittersweet, as a food source during the harsher months.

— *Chard deNiord*

Hermit Thrush

The hermit thrush is set for six
to sing her song, as if it were
the end of the world and she was stirred
by dusk to sing the same sweet song
again and again in the understory,
as if to say, it's neither words
nor meaning that matter in the end
but the quality of sound, as if we
were deafened by the sun and needed
her song as a key to unlock our ears,
to hear and hear and understand,

to see and see, knowing that this
one day is the end for now,
which it is, *it is,* she claims, with a song
just loud enough to pierce the woods
until the night descends like a thousand
veils, and then just one.

Northern Goshawk *Accipiter gentilis*

HABITAT AND RANGE: A true symbol of wild places, goshawks are rarely found close to human disturbance. They require large, intact tracts of mature forests in which to set up their breeding territories. Rare and declining, their range in North America extends from the Appalachians, north across the boreal forest of the northern United States and Canada, and down the Rocky Mountains into Mexico. Some individuals will migrate south for the winter, but the majority remain in the northern latitudes year-round.

DESCRIPTION AND NOTES: A huge raptor, their rounded wings and long tail make them adept at maneuvering among tree trunks, permitting them to hunt in even the densest forests. The adults are gray above with a white breast that is heavily barred with black. The adult birds have a distinctive, almost glowing, red eye. Fiercely territorial, goshawks are infamous for their aggressive behavior around nests, often diving on anyone who comes too close. They hunt large prey; grouse and snowshoe hare are both staples in their diet. Despite their large size and aggressive behavior, goshawks can be extremely difficult to find. They are spread thin across the landscape, and any sighting of this denizen of the wilderness should be considered special indeed. Goshawks are declining rapidly in the Northern Appalachians. Their need for large hunting territories meant there were never too many goshawks occupying the region, but the number of nests has been decreasing over the years. No single cause is known, but it is thought that the mosquito-borne, West Nile virus might be a culprit.

— *George David Clark*

Northern Goshawk

I dreamed I knew the forest
    through a keen,

red eye, and nothing moved
    except the snow

like braided curtains
    in the sky. The genes

that kink a gnarly length
    of mistletoe

around an oak's black neck,
          that plot and row

the hemlocks in their maze
          of ice-choked green,

that twist and craze and finally
          knot—those genes,

in me, were churning winds
          that couldn't blow

until, until a feathered
          quickness far below

adjusted slightly
          and the snarl came clean.

I was gone before
          I knew to go,

a nimble plunging
          and a wry careen,

the live embodiment
          of vertigo.

And the snow fell heavy
          in a whirling screen.

the bigger, fiercer, wilder relative of the Sharp-shinned
short, broad wings and a long rudderlike tail that give
superb aerial agility. These secretive birds are mostly g
flash through forests and mammal prey, ch
pouncing silently first through brush
grab quarry in talons. Falconers hav
trained goshawks thousand years
pairs build and maintain alternate nests
options available, they year afte
year, or may switch to a
add fresh conifer needle
Aromatic chemicals in
natural insecticide and
well known for its fierce
alternate short flights
as they search for prey, and
quickly and silently, strike
reckless hunters fly at high
occasionally stalk prey on foot
capture mammals more than
sky dance as part of their court
fly together in an undulating
vocal when defending their nest
human intruders and kill neighb
including owls and hawks. Your
finding a Northern Goshawk is to time
mature forest being as quiet, obser and pat
In some years, perhaps when pr
north, autumn invasions may hawks
short bursts of amazingly fast
among branches and crashing thickets
the intensity of pursuit. Northe hawks can
found in both deciduous and forest
normally only vocalize during
always found solitarily or

Red-eyed Vireo *Vireo olivaceus*

HABITAT AND RANGE: Red-eyed vireos are a common breeder in mature, deciduous forest stands with closed canopies. Found throughout the Appalachians, their breeding range extends from the southeastern United States, north to Canada, and down the Rocky Mountains. They leave the region in winter, migrating south to the Amazon basin. During migration they may be encountered in a variety of habitats, frequently joining feeding flocks with other bird species.

DESCRIPTION AND NOTES: Like many songbirds, red-eyed vireos are heard more often than seen. Among all the Appalachian breeding species, no bird sings more frequently than the red-eyed vireo. Vireos fill the forest with their incessant "Here-I-am, Where-are-you?" songs late into the summer afternoons when other birds have fallen silent. A single male can sing for hours at a time, sometimes repeating its song thousands of times throughout the day. It is not the most striking bird when seen—pale-olive above and white below with a black eyeline. The namesake eye color can be difficult to see without a good vantage. Red-eyed vireo nests are one of the most frequently parasitized forest species by the brown-headed cowbird. Cowbirds locate vireo nests, lay one of their eggs in it when the vireo adults are not present, and leave the egg for the vireos to hatch and raise as their own. The red-eyed vireo has a stable population in our region. Its main threats are logging operations that destroy breeding habitat.

— *Ryan Walsh*

Red-eyed Vireo

> I am alarmed when it happens that I have walked a mile into the woods bodily, without getting there in spirit.
> —HENRY DAVID THOREAU, "Walking"

Voice of summer
high in your canopy
I know you by ear
most common bird
of my home range
Swannanoa to Codding Hollow
your song rings out
from the first cool light of spring
through deepest August swelter

spilling from the broad leaves
constant as a brook in season

Field guides call your
song monotonous
tireless persistent
but I too know the need to be
asking and answering
the same spare question

Here I am! Where are you?

We assign words to shape
meaning and remember
making syllables from sounds
notes repeating like a kind of
koan, some green mantra
from deep in the trees

Here I am. Where are you?

Not in my senses
attention trailing my steps
like a shadow most days
preoccupied distracted
a mile or more along the path
before I'm awake

Here I am. Where are you?

A ringing bell
20,000 times a day
If I listen even once
I'll arrive here yes here
mind and body keeping pace
and the spirit? Just this
steam rising from a patch of moss
in the bare morning light

V — Reptiles and Amphibians

Common Five-lined Skink *Plestiodon fasciatus*

HABITAT AND RANGE: This lizard is widely distributed in the central and eastern United States from the Gulf states to the Canadian border and into Ontario. It is common throughout the Northern Appalachians but absent from Massachusetts, New Hampshire, and Maine. Five-lined skinks prefer humid woodlands with springs, wetlands, or streams nearby. They frequent rocky areas, fallen trees, decayed logs, tree slashings, slab wood, mulch and firewood piles, backyard decks, and landscaping. Leaf litter provides habitat for small invertebrate prey, and sunlit areas close to hiding cover are essential for basking.

DESCRIPTION AND NOTES: They are a medium-sized skink, reaching maximum lengths of approximately eight inches, with five light-colored lines on the back and sides of a charcoal-colored, gray, or black body. The dorsolateral stripe is located on the third and fourth scales counting from the middle of the back. Male skinks develop red-orange coloration on the head and neck during the breeding season and can be very aggressive toward other males. Courtship behavior consists primarily of males pursuing females via scent trailing. Breeding takes place in May. Skinks lay four to twelve or more eggs under rocks, bark, and in rotting logs but do not cover them with nest material. Instead, the female stays near the eggs to protect and tend them. Once they hatch, young are left to fend for themselves. Juveniles display a blue tail that serves to direct predatory attention away from vital organs. During a potential predation event, the tail can be sacrificed and regrown, thus preserving the life of the skink. Five-lined skinks are an important component of the forest floor ecology and are most visible to human observers during the spring months when they leave cover to bask in the warming sun. Basking is necessary to maintain proper body temperatures, metabolic rates, and overall health.

— *Jeff Gundy*

The Skink Poem

> Male reproductive success is often limited by the ability to acquire mates; therefore, males have evolved strategies to mate with multiple females.
>
> In contrast, the number of offspring a female produces is generally not limited by the quantity of sexual partners; thus, selection for multiple matings is expected to be weaker than in males.
>
> —ZACHARY W. BATESON, JOHN D. KRENZ, and ROBERT E. SORENSEN, "Multiple Paternity in the Common Five-lined Skink (*Plestiodon fasciatus*)"

1.

Skink mating strategies are gender-specific, or so Bateson,
Krenz & Sorenson believe. In other ways the five-lined skinks

resemble us as well: they breathe and hear and see,
they eat and defecate, they tend their young.

2.

I doubt I will ever spend my days in the fragrant rotting woods,
my dazzle-blue tail like a flag, skittering through logs and leaves,

over and under, hungry sometimes, sometimes stuffed
on spiders or crickets, termites, snails, fast as anything

but willing in a pinch to ditch my tail and scurry,
with any luck confusing my captor for just long enough.

3.

When there are eggs I mind them, guard them,
as best I can. As for the stories that cats have eaten

our tails and sickened, even died, why would
we skinks desire to spread such odious rumors?

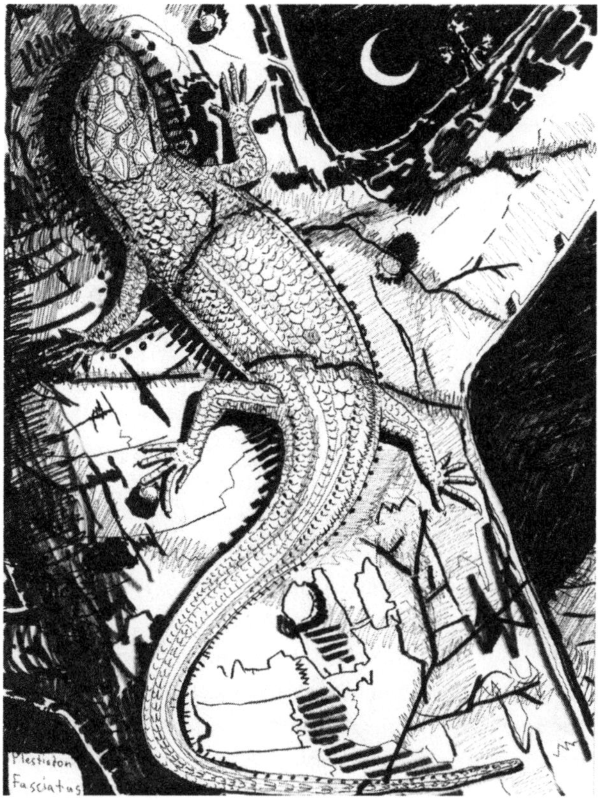

4.

And now the pond reveals how old I am—my head
a yellow-orange bright as an autumn sugar maple.

I cannot smile. Do I wish to smile,
deep in my skinkish self? Do I wish at all?

5.

I have my ways, and they are older than yours,
and I do not need you to blunder into them

and break what you do not understand.
But it may still be that I need you.

Eastern Milk Snake *Lampropeltis t. triangulum*

HABITAT AND RANGE: The eastern milk snake is distributed from the lower Mississippi valley through the Great Lakes States along the Appalachian Range through New England to southern Maine. This species has adapted well to human habitation and prefers old fields, meadows, woodland edges, power line rights-of-way, rocky slopes, rock walls, wood piles, slab piles, and old foundations of houses and barns. If there are milk snakes in the area and concrete slabs exist, they will likely be found nearby.

DESCRIPTION AND NOTES: The eastern milk snake is a medium-sized, nonvenomous snake ranging in length from twenty-four to forty inches. Their body color is tan or light gray with rusty-red- to mahogany-colored oblong blotches aligned crossways down the back and sides, each outlined with a thick black line. The head is narrow, and individuals have a uniquely shaped, lengthwise blotching pattern. The white belly has a checkerboard pattern of dark rectangles that span its width. This species is often confused with the venomous northern copperhead and is needlessly killed. However, there are several identifying characteristics that distinguish the two species. Milk snakes have round pupils, a checkerboard belly pattern, and the underside of the tail has two rows of scales. Copperheads have vertically elliptical pupils, blotches on the belly that are confined to the edges of the belly and do not span its width, and the underside of the tail has a single row of scales. Milk snakes have smooth scales, creating a shiny, wet-look appearance compared to a copperhead whose keeled scales appear dry and velvety. Mating takes place in the spring, and in June or July up to twenty-five eggs are laid under flat rocks, bark, and in rotted logs or mulch piles. Milk snakes eat mice and voles as well as frogs, salamanders, and insects. This is a mild-mannered snake, which will rarely attempt to bite if handled properly.

— *David Shumate*

Milk Snake

As the snake slithers down the inside of the chimney, avoiding the birch bark flames I have kindled, that ancient instinct returns, and I grab the fireplace poker to skewer it. But then the snake curls up in the corner. As if to render itself invisible. A feeling I know all too well.

Each year we find the skins they've shed in the attic of this century-old cabin. Where bats roost by day and swarm out to hunt at night. The old fables claimed that milk snakes nursed from the udders of cows. Though my grandfather, a dairy farmer all his life, scoffed at such a silly notion.

Loons . . . Sandhill cranes . . . Cormorants. All members of my own mythology. Who come to me in my dreams. With lessons I need to learn. And now this snake. Who I grasp with the fireplace tongs, lift aloft and carry writhing to the barrel whose lid my wife is holding like a gong.

We drive down Zulich Trail and stop at the cedar grove where a friend who likes his whiskey a little too much once claimed to have seen a pair of elves mating. There we tip the barrel and spill the snake into the grass. It hesitates. As if we've become part of some parable. Those old stories we tell over and over again. Embellishing them along the way. Never straying too far from the truth.

This time, again—a man, a woman, a snake. Maybe you've heard it before? They used to call it *The Fall*. Though in this version, we dispense with all the small talk—apples . . . promises . . . desires. I just nudge the snake deeper into the grass with my cane. And we return, in silence, to the cabin. Our breakfast now cold in the skillet. Our fire only embers in the hearth.

Northern Dusky Salamander *Desmognathus f. fuscus*

HABITAT AND RANGE: Northern dusky salamanders occur from South Carolina through Maine, into Quebec and New Brunswick, and are extremely common throughout the Appalachian range. They live in and along the edges of small streams both intermittent and perennial. They can also be found in spring seeps. Forested areas are preferred due to shade, which moderates water and soil temperatures and facilitates wet conditions.

DESCRIPTION AND NOTES: Northern dusky salamanders range in length from two and a half to five and a half inches and can be tan, brown, or almost black, especially in older adults. They have a triangular tail, which is useful in distinguishing this species from the similarly appearing mountain dusky salamander, which has a rounded tail. Northern dusky salamanders usually display a light eye stripe, which extends from the corner of the eye to the corner of the mouth. Examining from above, northern duskies have a broad brown or tan stripe, which runs down their back. The edges of this stripe are scalloped or wavy rather than straight as in the mountain dusky. They consume earthworms, aquatic invertebrates, and insects and are preyed upon primarily by fish and raccoons. Courtship occurs on land during the summer and results in the female picking up a spermatophore deposited onto the substrate by the male. Females attach up to thirty eggs to the underside of rocks, logs, bark, or clumps of moss. They curl up around the eggs and guard them until hatching, which occurs in forty to sixty days. The larvae have external gills and transform into subadults in approximately nine months. This common species is widely distributed and can be locally abundant in smaller headwater streams. It is an important indicator of water quality, disappearing when silt, sediment, mine drainage, or acid precipitation degradation occurs.

— *Jordan Temchack*

Northern Dusky Salamander, A Prayer

> In dwelling, live close to the ground.
> —LAO-TZU

Might've mistaken him for God,
but this was not
my first encounter
with a being of supreme
physical stature.

One lives in danger
of treating every sensation
like rapture,
if one is controlled by fear.

A man lifts
my abode
(a massive river stone)
like an oak leaf.

Air
flushes
through
my body—
quick,
hot,
& raw
—as sunlight
burns my skin.

Peeling
my eyelids open,
I greet him
with stillness.

I feel him
watching over me,
I'm overwhelmed
by the lack
of obstruction:
the singing
of the stream,
the groaning
bark against
branches,
I sense
the warm breath
of wind
washing
leaves & limbs . . .

In thinking,
keep to the simple.

When you are content to be
simply yourself
& don't compare
or compete,
everybody will respect you.

This is my prayer,
my offering,
as this man
holds my life in his hands!

A humble home
held overhead
by shaky arms
casts a dusky-shadow—
rain clouds
carrying the weight
of a continent.

Northern Ring-necked Snake *Diadophis punctatus edwardsii*

HABITAT AND RANGE: This subspecies is widely distributed from northern Alabama and northern Georgia through the Great Lakes states to Maine and eastern Canada. It is very common in the Northern Appalachian region. A habitat generalist, it prefers drier, upland habitats in mountainous areas, along utility rights-of-way, talus slopes, along field and road edges, and in basements and buildings. It is often associated with flat rocks.

DESCRIPTION AND NOTES: This small to medium-sized, smooth-scaled, nonvenomous snake reaches adult lengths of twelve to twenty-four inches with a black or bluish-black back and a light belly with matching ring around the neck. The belly color can range from almost white to a pale yellow, deep yellow, or orange yellow. Vividly contrasting colors make this a visually appealing snake. It has a uniformly long slender body, with larger specimens usually not exceeding one-half inch in body diameter. Due to its distinctive color pattern and descriptive name, this is one of the easiest snakes to identify. Mating occurs during the spring. The female lays one to six oblong eggs approximately one-quarter inch in diameter and one and a half inches in length. Eggs are laid under flat rocks, bark slabs, or in rotting logs and incubate for forty-five to sixty days. At hatching, neonate ring-necked snakes are between four and six inches long and less than one-quarter inch in diameter. This species eats insects—such as beetles, grubs, crickets, invertebrates, worms—and small amphibians, including juvenile frogs and salamanders. Northern ring-necked snakes are often found in basements and buildings but are completely harmless to humans.

— *Susan Barba*

Diadophis punctatus edwardsii

Secretive and seldom
encountered in the open,
inhabitant of the upper soil,
harmless, they say, and active
from April to October, found

along power-line easements,
scree fields and talus slopes,
along fire roads,
in building basements,
beneath stone slabs,
between porch risers,

in the twilight zones of caves,
inside junk piles,
in sodden logs,
in lowlands and floodplains,
wherever moisture is present
below the moldering leaves,

and higher in drier reaches,
beside roadcuts,
beside Skyline Drive
in the Shenandoah,
Beech Cliffs in Acadia,
beneath beech forests'
marcescent murmuring,

also called
Collared snake,
fodder snake,
king snake,
ring snake,
little black-and-red snake,

Diadophis punctatus,
named for its headband
and ventral spotting,
edwardii, to honor the Englishman,
surname Edward,
who painted and published
an uncommon
history of birds, who
must have watched
and waited many hours
to see them,

the way one must
to see a snake
who prefers to move
its blue black slender
body through the world
unseen, seeking the sun
to warm its blood,
like any animal in spring
when it's bright and cold,
uncoiling.

Pickerel Frog *Lithobates palustris*

HABITAT AND RANGE: Pickerel frogs are widespread from Texas through the mid-South up through the Great Lakes states and from Alabama and Georgia north through Maine and eastern Canada. They are very common throughout Northern Appalachia. They are best described as a meadow frog as that is their preferred habitat. They also inhabit swamps, slow-moving streams, lake margins, small ponds, and backwaters.

DESCRIPTION AND NOTES: Pickerel frogs reach lengths of up to three and a half inches. Their body has a base color of cream or tan with large, squarish brown spots on the head and back that are generally outlined in black and aligned in two rows between the dorsolateral ridges. In contrast, the less common northern leopard frog—(a commonly confused species)—has spots that are round, not aligned in rows, and are outlined with light halos. Pickerel frogs are yellow or orange on the belly and on the inside of the legs. A pickerel frog's coloration is ideally suited for hiding and hunting in waving grasses and dappled sunlight. Pickerel frogs are a very common species in a variety of habitats, which makes them important as both prey and predator. They primarily eat insects and in turn are prey for wading birds, raccoons, mink, fish, and snakes. Pickerel frogs are very active on cool mornings when the sun is bright and the grass is wet from dew or rain. Breeding occurs during March through May. Males position themselves near or in the water. Vocalizations consist of a brief croak, or when issued from under water, a long, low-pitched call described as sounding like snoring. Mating occurs in the water, and up to three thousand eggs are deposited in a globular mass onto submerged vegetation. The eggs hatch in one to two weeks, and the tadpoles metamorphose in eighty-five to ninety-five days.

— *Julia Shipley*

Pickerel Frog

I'm the one whose cry sounds like *a finger on a balloon,*
 a short snore, a little growl, now that I've shimmed out
from the bottom ooze into wet meadows. Find me
 in thickets and ditches, an excellent jumper and leaper,
"'Once upon a time,' said Frog, 'there were two good friends,
 a frog and a toad,'" wrote Arnold Lobel,
omitting the blemished road. I'm the one whose cry
 sounds like *a finger on a balloon,* a short snore,

a little growl. When you leave your house on a foggy night
walking the lane for the annual herp count, primed
to find me among the newts and peepers, hunt for my
yellow waistcoat, rectangular spots. My friend, bring your spatula.

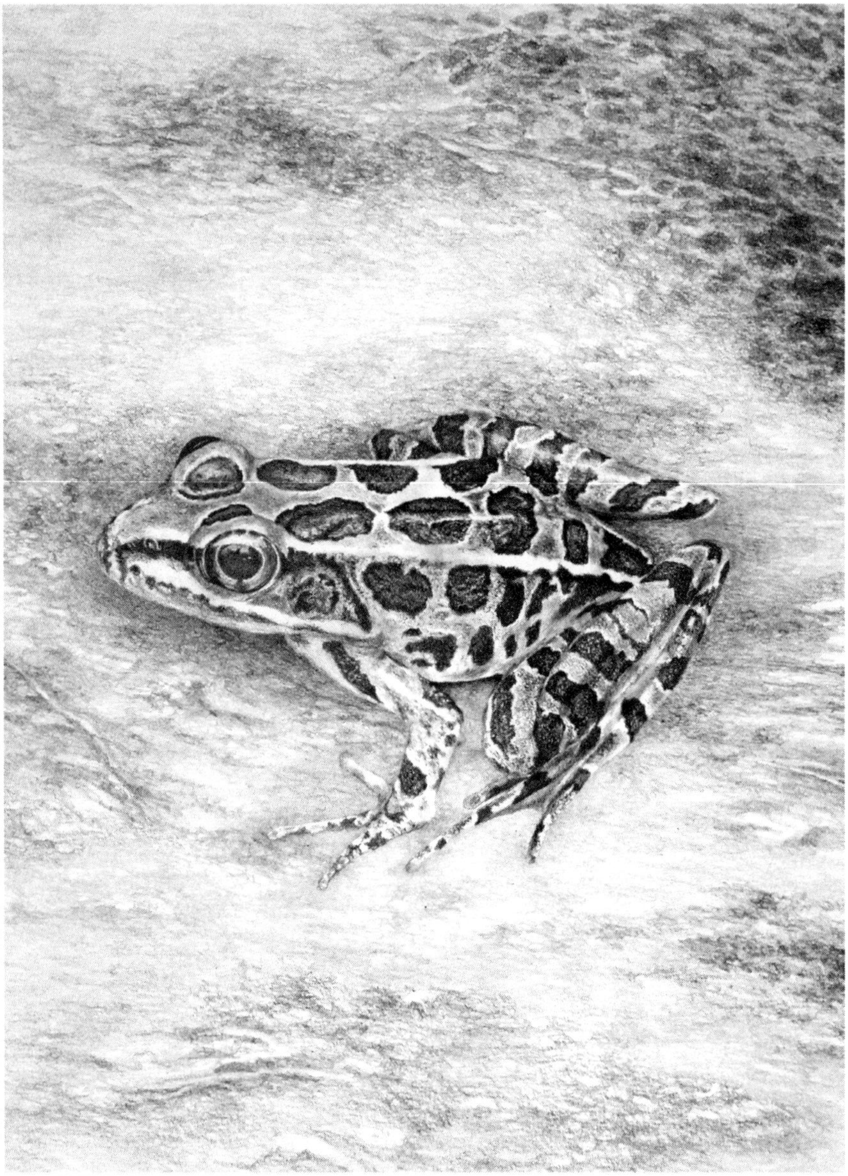

Red-backed Salamander *Plethodon cinereus*

HABITAT AND RANGE: Red-backed salamanders are one of the most widely distributed salamanders in eastern North America, ranging from North Carolina through eastern Canada and west to Minnesota. Red-backed salamanders are creatures of forested areas but do not need to be near or associated with flowing or standing water. Thus, they can occupy a wider range of forested habitats than many other salamander species. They are less abundant in wetlands, poorly drained soils, and especially coniferous woodlands, which they avoid due to acidic soils.

DESCRIPTION AND NOTES: This small woodland salamander reaches lengths of less than four inches and has a round tail. Aptly named with a red- or rust-colored broad stripe running down the back and sides that are gray or charcoal colored. A common color variation is the leadphase or leadback. Individuals with this coloration are typically gray or dark gray, and the red stripe is absent. The leadback color morph is quite common in some populations. Red-backed salamanders belong to the group of lungless salamanders. Respiration occurs primarily through the skin and requires adequate soil moisture found in habitats with intact forest canopy, wet leaves, damp soil, and decomposing logs. Density estimates of red-backed salamanders suggest they are frequently the most abundant vertebrate in a given area. Thus, its role in the food web and as a foundation species is very important. It preys upon mites, spiders, millipedes, numerous insects, and other small invertebrates. In turn, snakes prey upon them. Wild turkeys occasionally find and opportunistically consume them when scratching through the leaf litter for seeds and nuts.

— *Michael Garrigan*

Red-backed Salamander

A slender sumpter of soil
crawls from a seep in the earth—
the morning dew dripping from wood fern
the moistness clinging to every dark thing.

Nestling in the soft cavity of a decaying ash,
it reads the Emerald borers death script, waiting
for the ground to cool, for shade to cover its steps.
Hemlocks fall and under their hard bellies, spiders.

Gorging on mosquitoes still in their soft sacks
clinging to silent slack water; its back streaked
by the blood of box elder bark is the only scream
as it searches the shadows of stinging nettle.

Myths crumble under tiny toes scurrying
across silver maple leaves cradling its stories
into rivulets of dirt, rock and stick.   Listen.
Trace these skittering paths to the unseen.

HABITAT AND RANGE: Wood frogs are widely distributed in woodlands from Alabama and Georgia through Maine to eastern Canada, up through the midwestern United States, and across most Canadian provinces to Alaska. It prefers mature timber along streams, temporary ponds, and areas near wetlands. Wet meadows and damp wooded areas with sunlit openings are favored foraging and basking areas.

DESCRIPTION AND NOTES: Wood frogs reach lengths of around three inches, and their bodies are usually tan but can be rusty red or grayish. Their most distinctive feature is the black or dark brown, "raccoon-like" mask extending from the eyes toward the shoulder. They have a distinctive dorsolateral ridge, and the snout is pointed. Tadpoles are dark brown and easily identified by a high, ridged crest on the tail and a gold-speckled belly. Wood frogs are the first frog to emerge and breed in the spring and require fishless, temporary ponds for successful reproduction. They become active in March–May, when nighttime air temperatures reach fifty degrees Fahrenheit. Warm rains cause large numbers of frogs to move toward breeding ponds where males call in choruses akin to the sound of quacking ducks or a flock of turkeys. Mating occurs in the water, and large, floating, globular masses of up to two thousand eggs are deposited and hatch in approximately three weeks. The tadpoles metamorphose in sixty to seventy days. Wood frogs are ambush predators and change hunting locations based on ground moisture, sun angles, and prey availability. They eat insects, worms, and small invertebrates. Wood frogs overwinter in leaf litter, under logs, and on the edges of wetlands and seeps. They can survive in subzero temperatures because increased glucose levels act as an antifreeze in their blood and tissues. Acid precipitation has decreased the pH in many forested, temporary ponds, making them unsuitable for wood frog egg and larval survival.

— *Sarah Blake*

Late Night Talks with the Wood Frog

Wood frog, I do not envy your ability to route your urine to your blood stream.
I do not envy the cells drinking it up. The cells allowed to die
partly—
a recoverable amount.

We don't often talk about the amount of death
we can come back from.

If someone doesn't die, we don't know how much they *did* die.

My mother—if at some point, she had recovered, they would not have told us, *She died 60%.*

We're not studied so precisely.

The tumors are studied more than the female bodies they inhabit, more than your frog body.

You—to life again—

someone thought, *The physiological mechanisms at work here are knowable.*
Glucose pumped out by the liver, combining with the urine, preserving
the cell,
in the extreme cold.

I know, I know. You're chiding me—we can know a lot about a tumor and not
know how to fix it.

Your body saw the near-death as an acceptable amount.

Glory be. The intention of your species to procreate was not inhibited.
You need not migrate

or build fires or climb your permeable

af skin under piles and piles of furs. Your body adapted. Your body
solved it another way.

Wood Turtle *Glyptemys insculpta*

HABITAT AND RANGE: The wood turtle occurs from Virginia through Maine and the Great Lakes states. The largest densities are found in Pennsylvania. This woodland turtle may also be found in swamps, marshes, bogs, and wet pastures. They are normally found not far from water. However, during the summer, some individuals may roam a mile or more away from their wintering habitat. They overwinter by submerging in slow-moving streams, pools, or backwaters from October to April or May.

DESCRIPTION AND NOTES: Also known as "woods turtle" and "redlegs turtle," they are a medium-sized turtle with a seven to nine-inch, keeled, brown carapace (top shell). Growth rings are significantly raised on the scutes (shell scales), creating an appearance of a sculpted or carved shell. The rear margin of the carapace is flared upward in adults, and the plastron (bottom shell) is yellow or orange with black blotches on each scute. The skin is dark brown except on the turtle's underside and areas normally protected by the shell where it is orange to red in color; hence, the nickname of "redlegs turtle." Wood turtles eat a variety of plants and animals, including berries, vegetation, earthworms, and other invertebrates. Mating occurs in water, and four to eighteen eggs are laid in well-drained soil during May to July. Eggs not predated by raccoons, skunks, or other predators hatch in forty to sixty-seven days. Wood turtles are declining due to illegal overcollecting and habitat destruction. Requiring both terrestrial and aqueous habitats means that losses of either habitat type can be sufficient to eliminate a wood turtle population. They are protected from legal harvest throughout most of their range, but the illegal pet trade has had a devastating effect on wood turtle populations in some areas of their range.

— *Henry Walters*

Psychopomp

Rouse him. It takes
a certain tact.   Art of some kind.
Seasoning.   Like sounding for
a silent thing.   As to raise Lazarus,
knock at the door   of every tomb.
(By *raise* I mean   *recall to mind.*)
To restart the heart,
raise it like   bone artifact
from river mud   where oxygen's thin
as Everest's: not to be sipped,
to be ambered in.

There's life above
& before & below the room we know.
(By *room* I mean *this half-lit cave*
that molds & maps how river or time
or poem behaves.)
Warden of season,
raise your head. Heave onto this raft
of shore. Shoulder through wet wallows
of tightly scrolled ostrich ferns,
trout lilies, lattice of beaver-coppiced
pussywillow. You cover ground
at a century's pace. Gray as a glacial
boulder above, red as Euphrates
clay below, older than either—
by *older* I mean *over & after*—
you raise the scutes of your vaulted ribs
concentrically, course upon course
of ziggurat, like contour lines
of a white pine's age.
In you, time's gauge,
the built world roots & bivouacs
as though the very dream of such
armorial stratigraphy
could carry us. Through human sod
& kingdoms lost we rise blind
as nightcrawlers drawn to the thumps
of your practiced feet, a Doric order
of columns raised to a Pleistocene god
without a name.
Worm charmer,
freshwater diviner, you sound like rain
stampeding through our burial ground
whose glyphs & ghosts are scoured down
to afterthought. At the ancient site
of your cold-blooded bed we bow our heads
beneath the shell of the still intact
original lintel, magnificent
worn pediment toward which we raise
ourselves as if in praise of all
emergent life.

VI ~ Fish

American Eel *Anguilla rostrata*

HABITAT AND RANGE: A catadromous species, it lives in freshwater until maturity and migrates to the Sargasso Sea in the Atlantic Ocean to spawn. Eels ascend watersheds via rivers that enter the Gulf of Mexico and the western Atlantic Ocean from Florida to the northernmost reaches of Atlantic Canada and the St. Lawrence River to Lake Ontario.

DESCRIPTION AND NOTES: Nearly transparent larvae (glass eels) drift on ocean currents and grow to four to six inches long; pencil-sized, pigmented elvers (yellow eels) ascend coastal rivers in the spring. They can traverse nearly vertical, wetted surfaces on dam faces and along shorelines to get around obstacles. In freshwater, they spend five to twenty years maturing and may swim hundreds of miles inland to the uppermost headwaters. At maturity, they reach lengths of two to four feet, turn color again (silver eels), and begin a downstream, autumn journey to the Sargasso Sea. They are nocturnal and consume small invertebrates, crayfish, and small fish and are important prey for many fish species. They are the primary fish host for eastern elliptio freshwater mussels. Parasitic mussel larvae attach to the gills of American eels and hitch a ride upstream, sometimes around dams, before detaching and settling to the bottom. Declines in eastern elliptio mussels correspond to declines in American eels. American eels were an important food for Native Americans and settlers who built downstream-pointing, V-shaped weirs with hand-placed rocks to guide the fish as they migrated downstream in the fall. A fish collection device was located at the downstream end of the *V.* Remnants of these weirs can still be seen at river level and in aerial photos on major coastal rivers such as the Delaware, Susquehanna, and Juniata in Pennsylvania. Threats include water pollution and blockages to migration by dams. Restoration efforts include upstream eel passage devices, trap and transport of elvers to upstream areas, and improvement of downstream fish passage at hydroelectric dams.

— *Elizabeth Bradfield*

From Sea, toward Sea

for Rachel Carson, for Anguilla

Slippery, these selves, our origins. Out there,
new, at sea, we mingled, borderless. We hatched
from our own round worlds into currents

wafting sargassum's canopy. What were we? Undifferentiated
by sex, unaware of nation, adrift and hungry,
slight enough to be picked up by anything—

eddy, porbeagle, loggerhead (sister, uncle, mother)—
        and moved, despite objection, no matter our will. We were
                willow leaves tossing in wind too big to know

as anything other than *home*. Not even elvers. Then, in months
        of becoming, we tasted tongues of water, found our thirst,
                and picked one. You don't need to know

why. What I know: I needed another home
        from my born-to to become myself, so I followed
                what felt right. What water was sweetest, even

if strange. In mixed salt, in brine, half
        home half away, I writhed, vulnerable, and thrilled
                to transparency, so full of life my organs pulsed clear

through my skin. I am sorry for those who found me, who
        had to reckon with that naked and vulnerable joy. Then
                I let myself run. Ancestry both alive in me

and nothing. Upriver. Hundreds of miles against
        the pull I'd never, until now, tasted. Becoming
                she, me. That middling estuary of *maybe* not

enough. Up through runnels, over dams and, rain-slick nights, even
        across fields no one imagined I could survive, until the right water
                held me. The right, soft silt. I burrowed in, warm

in dark, warm through cold seasons, safe
        from summer's piercing shine. Years. Decades. Comfortable
                enough despite the dangers of others' hungers. Slick

and twisting in anyone's hands who tried to move me, slick
        in my own self, twined. I was satisfied. I grew. I won't tell you
                what I learned of desire, loss, season, or want. These

are near enough for you to know for yourself. And now. But
        now, despite me, my eyes shift toward a different seeing, grow
                larger and eager to see again in dim, deep light again. My body

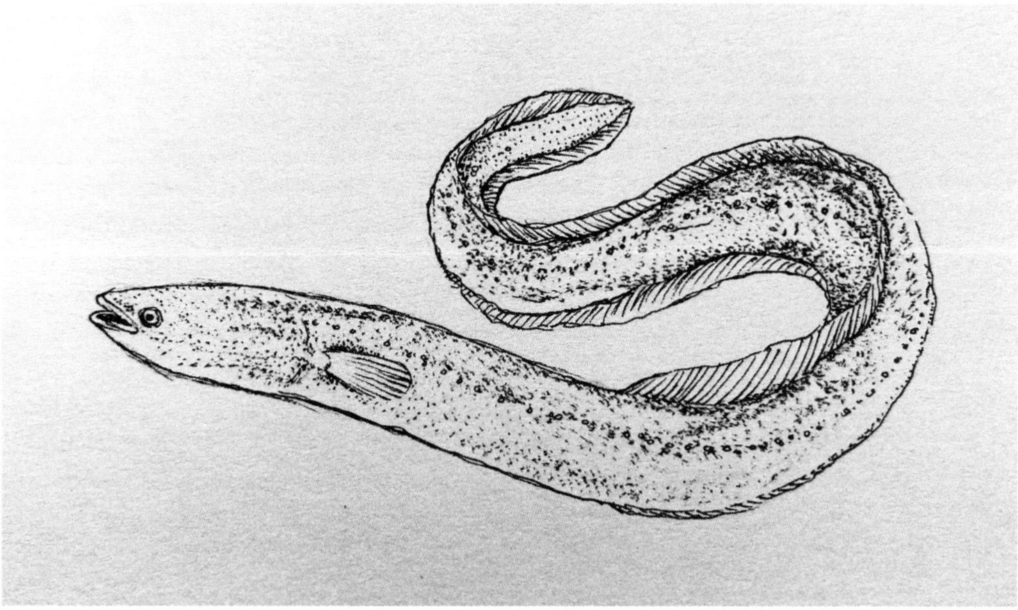

hungers for water that cannot hold me snug in banks but lets me
    loose again, again wildly alive and unnoticed or too small
        for notice or away from the shores (at last) of notice. I am

no salmon, after all. The ocean is origin and end, not middle
    jaunt. Start and finish of my wildest parts, the least known,
        where my body comes from, where it goes. I go.

American Shad *Alosa sapidissima*

HABITAT AND RANGE: This anadromous species spawns during the spring in rivers draining to the Atlantic Ocean from the St. Johns River in Florida through Nova Scotia. The largest runs occurred in the Susquehanna River in Maryland, Pennsylvania, and New York, before hydroelectric dams blocked access to upstream spawning areas. Currently, the strongest runs are on the Delaware, Connecticut, and Hudson Rivers. During the fall, juvenile shad migrate to the ocean and spend three to six years maturing, primarily in the Gulf of Maine. Adults return during March to June, often swimming hundreds of miles upstream to spawn.

DESCRIPTION AND NOTES: This member of the herring family has large, silvery scales and a metallic blue/olive and coppery sheen on their backs and flanks, respectively. They have deep, laterally compressed bodies, with sharp-edged scales on their bellies and deeply forked tails. Males average two to five pounds and females average four to six pounds, with occasional specimens exceeding seven to nine pounds. Unlike Pacific salmon, all American shad do not die after spawning. Up to 20 percent will go back to the ocean and return to spawn in a future year. Spawning occurs in early evening in large pools with males and females swimming and splashing in small schools just under the surface. Eggs are released and fertilized in the water column and must keep moving or lightly settle on substrate free of sediment and with adequate oxygen to hatch successfully. American shad consume aquatic insects in freshwater and plankton in the ocean. They were an important food for Native Americans. Known as the "poor man's salmon," an ongoing tradition of sport and commercial fishing dates back to colonial times. Historically, violent "shad wars" occurred on certain rivers as colonists fought over fishing rights. Modern threats to American shad include dams blocking access to spawning areas, water pollution, and poorly regulated bycatch in offshore areas. Many states and the federal government are actively involved in restoration efforts.

— *Gary Hawkins*

POEM (AMERICAN SHAD)

With time, my grief would always find others like himself, glimpsing mica eyes within somnolent subway passages or mindlessly trailing stronger specimens along sidewalks downtown—all of us like those fishes that school spaced out in the long line length of river, disguising ourselves as solitary, prodigal, and inconsequential among rocks. Though if you stand along shores at dusk you will see us everywhere, everywhere.

HABITAT AND RANGE: The brook trout's native distribution spans eighteen eastern states, from northeast Ohio eastward and from Georgia north through Maine and into Canada. Recent phylogenetic analyses suggest separate southern and northern strains. In the southern portion of Northern Appalachia, brook trout are primarily found in small, mountainous, first and second order, cold-water streams. In New England, they are also found in ponds, and medium to large lakes with adequate cold water to survive summer conditions.

DESCRIPTION AND NOTES: Known by various colloquial names such as "native," "speckled trout," "brook trout," "brook charr," and "squaretail," brook trout are correctly classified as a char rather than a trout, such as brown trout or rainbow trout. They are the apex predator in most headwater stream systems where they occur unless introduced trout or naturalized brown trout are also present. They share their habitat with blacknose dace, longnose dace, creek chubs, stonerollers, and various sculpin species. Further north and in larger waters, they commonly coexist with rainbow smelt, creek chubsuckers, and fallfish. Clean, cold water is essential for their existence and continued survival. As streams freeze over in the winter or warm in the summer, brook trout move around the watershed to find the most suitable living conditions. Stream connectivity impeded by dams, elevated culverts, pollution, or elevated water temperature zones can prevent populations from moving throughout stream systems during various portions of the year. Hemlock woolly adelgids have reduced coniferous cover in some areas causing streams to warm. Acid precipitation falling on low-buffering-capacity watersheds has dangerously reduced stream pH and eliminated brook trout from many streams and still waters. Climate change brings new threats of widespread water temperature increases and more frequent floods that negatively impact spawning success and fry survival. Brook trout have gained new popularity in recent years as anglers have discovered the challenges and rewards of "bluelining," the practice of finding small, often unnamed streams on maps and prospecting them for brook trout fishing opportunities.

— *Todd Davis*

The Last Hiding Places

When August drought wanders the mountain like a panting dog and yellow poplar leaves worry the creek thin, hike the crease to the limestone gash where this stream emerges from underground.

Beneath hemlock branches, water basins and brookies gather in the shadows.

Noll

Approach on bended knee and peer over the rim.

More than ten will fin in what little current remains.

Wormy etchings spine their backs, a way to disappear from kingfisher who fly overhead.

Last year's spawn washes flames across the bellies of these char.

Along their sides, blue and yellow halos circle a red the color of Icarus's heart in Matisse's painting.

If you told me that the story of the world's beginnings was brushed on the canvas of every scale and cell of these fish, I'd believe you.

If you're lucky, a hatch will begin, flies so small at first you can't see them.

Then a rise.

And another.

The gentle press of open mouths and arching backs dimple the surface.

As if the rain these fish desperately need has at last begun to fall.

HABITAT AND RANGE: Chain pickerel are a widespread species occurring from Florida to Nova Scotia. They are native to watersheds draining to the Gulf of Mexico, the Atlantic Ocean, and Lake Ontario. They prefer cool water and warm water lakes, ponds, swamps, beaver dams, low-gradient streams and rivers, and areas away from current with abundant submerged aquatic vegetation. Adults can range in length from sixteen to thirty inches with eighteen to twenty-two inches being typical of most adult specimens. They can be found across many habitat types in the Northern Appalachians, from lowland areas near tidal influence to small lakes, ponds, bogs, and mill dams at higher elevations.

DESCRIPTION AND NOTES: A member of the Esocid family, which includes northern pike and muskellunge, they have elongated bodies with dorsal and anal fins located rearward toward the tail. This adaptation enables those fins to increase the surface area of the tail region and provides significant thrust, thereby allowing them to dart out from weeds or cover to attack prey as it passes by. The "chain" portion of their name refers to the chainlike, horizontal, black lines against an olive body, which provides excellent camouflage as they sit stationary waiting for a feeding opportunity. They also have a prominent black "teardrop" running from their eye to the bottom of their jaw. Chain pickerel primarily feed on fish, frogs, and aquatic insects. They have numerous, large teeth on their jaws and a large number of rearward facing teeth on the roof of their mouth. They feed by biting most prey from the side and turning it headfirst to swallow it. The rearward facing teeth ensure few potential meals escape. They are a highly adapted, very efficient predator.

— *Willard P. Greenwood II*

There Was a Light on in the Country Church

Science knows small Chain Pickerel as hammer handles
But my brother and I used to call them (after a Calvin and Hobbes book),
Greenish and Cupreous Slime Creatures From Another Planet—
yet the two foot pickerel that I keelhauled
Into a resident canoe from the black stillwater
Of the actual Stillwater River
Was more akin to half a Peavey handle.
We pulled this being from under the cedar overhang
where the old railroad bed sank into the riverbank.
The silent local cemetery atop the ridge

Oversaw this whole scene—
I said don't touch it— but he reached to help
And the thrashing fish drove hooks into his fingers
And he and the fish fought.
    We were hunting these fish on a dreamy fall evening.
    Chain Pickerel won't fillet well because of the Y bones.
    We'd bake the whole fish and lift out the spine for our mom to make fish cakes.
    And in our later years, we'd dine on those with a deluxe pilsner
    And backyard garden Cole slaw.
On this juvenile evening,
I released the fish into the Vallisneria and Pickerel Weed Beds that
Grew out of a century's worth of logging bark
And beached my impaled brother in the old gravel pit.
I needed help, like in an after school special,
And left him there in the cold and getting colder dusk.
There would be no fish dinner tonight
But there was a light at the far end of the riverside
graveyard, and that's where I ran.

HABITAT AND RANGE: This species occupies watersheds draining to the Atlantic Ocean from Georgia to Canada. They are found in high-gradient, headwater streams, frequently in association with longnose dace, sculpins, and native brook trout. They can also be found in transitional streams where seasonal water temperatures blend between the cold water needed by trout and warmer waters associated with lower elevations and gradients. This may be the most common fish species in the Northern Appalachian range.

DESCRIPTION AND NOTES: This is one of the most recognizable and common fish species in headwaters and small streams throughout Appalachia. This small minnow reaches two to four inches in length and has a tan- or olive-colored back and white to cream-colored belly punctuated by a prominent, wide, black stripe running midflank from the tip of the nose through the eye to the base of the tail. Trout anglers often use them for bait, and they are known by popular nicknames such as "redfins" and "butter bellies" due to colors they display during the spring spawning season. They consume aquatic insects, small invertebrates, and vegetative material. Like brook trout, they can be absent from an otherwise suitable stream due to acidification from acid precipitation or acid mine drainage (AMD). They are one of the first species to recolonize following implementation of successful AMD abatement programs.

— *Nik Moore*

To the Blacknose Dace

When we hike, my sister's kids descend
    each gorge in search of water. The stream's
silver tail flicks in and out of sight and,
    like famished fish lured to the keenly
fashioned fly, the children dart.

In the water, the boys' jeans rolled up,
    the baby naked, they set themselves
to trapping, over-eager and over-sure
    of what they can take for themselves.

Each time a pair of their small hands
    lurches beneath the surface
I think of you. I want to tell you,

Go
where water blackens rock,
quick and low, shallow corner
of respite cloaked from sun,
from brook trout and hunger.
Though you, too, are hungry,
famished in a season of making,
your lateral stripe gone russet
in a show of virility and intention.
You could live a life of bait
though you, too, are baited.
Baited to the agile Connecticut
or a lower Ohio, Little Miami.
Or to the cupped and gentle hands
of my expectant nephew in search
of the crawdad. He knows of you
and of your likeness, flies tied
in homage to that enticing silver
sway, that busy dart, that black flag
along the body extending from a frown.
Show yourself to the child and flee.
Know, somehow, that my nephew
has some luck pulling critters
from streams. That on rare days
he might gather you from your
shady pool. Grateful just to have
something alive in his palm,
know that he will look you over
in the rapidly draining aquarium
of his hands, will take in your
simple silver shine, then lower
you. Release. Move on.
On such days, return to yourself
beneath the stacked creek shale.
Be with the crawdad who, too, hides
from the child. Who, too, knows
what it is to be brief
in water's longevity.

HABITAT AND RANGE: This large minnow species reaches twelve to sixteen inches and is native to medium-sized streams and larger rivers from the James River in Virginia through Maine and into eastern Ontario, New Brunswick, and Hudson Bay. They are primarily found in watersheds draining to the Atlantic Ocean but also are found in some watersheds draining to Lake Ontario. They prefer riffles and pools with sand, gravel, and rubble substrates.

DESCRIPTION AND NOTES: Fallfish have large scales and are silvery in appearance, except during the spring spawning season when males develop numerous small bumps (tubercles) on their heads and display reddish/coppery cheeks and flanks with dark gray backs. In advance of spawning, males build large nests by carrying gravel and small stones in their forward-facing mouths with thickened lips. These circular nests can be three to five feet in diameter and raised off the river bottom by six to ten inches. Other species of fish use the altered river bottom as resting and feeding areas. Eventually, flooding flows disperse the nest before the next spawning season. Fallfish coexist with trout in transitional stream sections and cold water rivers. In warmer rivers, they may be found in similar habitats as smallmouth bass. Fallfish eat a variety of insects, invertebrates, fish, and vegetation. They are often caught by anglers targeting gamefish who enjoy the strike and fight until realizing they have hooked a fallfish rather than a more glamorous species. Yet their abundance and willingness to strike artificial lures and flies has created fans among anglers who accept them without prejudice. In the northern reaches of their distribution, such as Maine, truly large fallfish exceeding eighteen inches have been caught. While generally underappreciated by humans, they are an important species, occupying the middle level of river food webs.

— *Joseph J. Capista*

Thinking Now and Again, at Age 46, of the Fallfish

O little denizen of cataclysm
dwelling best where water falls
to other water and for whom
safekeeping's safest keeping
is perpetual foment,
                    o silver
architect whose pebble nests
revise eternal current's line
yet are, by that same current,
also revised,

o *most colossal*
native minnow—as notes each
field guide on my shelf—our
tacit paradox who's steady
amid eddies, undercurrents
unseen and unforeseen, I ask
you now:
how might I, midstream
in middle age, my world a rush
of cloudburst-muddied water
that once ran clear as dew,

ever know the endless wild sky
from heron's underbelly of blue?

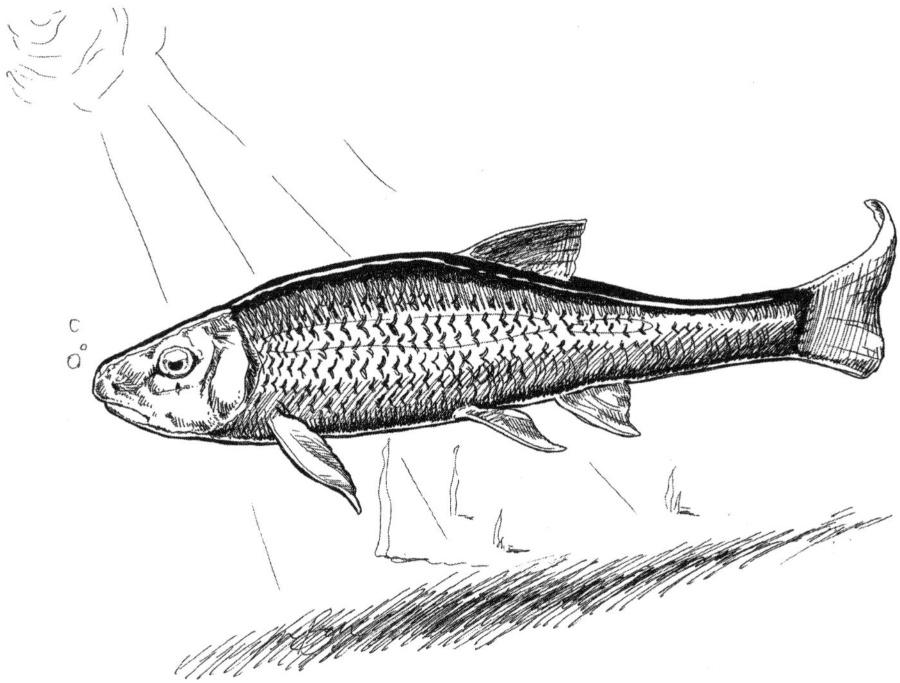

HABITAT AND RANGE: The landlocked salmon is an inland, non-oceangoing variety of the Atlantic salmon. Landlocks live in clean, cold water lakes and rivers in the northeastern United States and eastern Canadian provinces. They have been stocked in the Great Lakes, cold water reservoirs, lakes, and river systems from New Jersey north through New England. Lake and riverine populations both require river and stream habitats for successful spawning.

DESCRIPTION AND NOTES: The species name *salar* originates from Latin meaning "leap." Landlocked and oceangoing Atlantic salmon are renowned for their leaping ability needed to navigate past waterfalls during upstream migrations. The landlocked portion of their name denotes that the riverine subspecies (*ouananiche*) and the lake subspecies (*sebago*) neither leave freshwater nor travel to the ocean. Instead, a lake, pond, or larger river system serves as their permanent home. Naturally occurring populations of landlocks originated from migratory, oceangoing populations, and their original distribution aligns with watersheds draining to the North Atlantic Ocean. Landlocked salmon in lakes feed on rainbow smelt, chubs, smaller trout, and aquatic invertebrates and may reach average weights of four to eight pounds. In river systems, they also consume dace, chubs, fallfish, and sculpins; however, aquatic insects form a larger portion of their diet, and average sizes are smaller, averaging from one to four pounds. While popular wherever they are found, landlocks in Maine have a devout following. Many wilderness sporting camps developed in the late 1800s to provide access to these fish for wealthy anglers from major eastern cities. Infrastructure—such as train routes, float planes, and the development of state parks and natural areas—was created in response to the angling publics' desire to pursue these fish. Their willingness to take an artificial fly, a propensity to jump when hooked, and the wilderness settings in which they are found, make this an iconic New England sportfish.

— *Henry Hughes*

Landlocked Salmon

Ice Age wanderer, swimming seams of rising rock,
the melting salt sheets of Earth's late morning.
Marooned long ago by the flood-gouged rivers
as they shut to the sea, you're a glacial erratic

in the granite bed of Sebago. With April's icy breakup,
you raid the smelt shallows, then drop like mercury
under summer's tasty thermocline
until fall bronzes you up-creek to spawn.

Not such a bad life: a forest-ringed pool, cold and clear.
No orcas, seals, or sharks. No Greenland drift nets.
Just anglers casting and trolling for the leaping
landlocks they love. But what do you know of love

or loss? Black speckled, sterling bolt, magnetically
tilted to sea. A faint whiff of briny krill.
The silver ghosts of your ancestors
vanishing in the warming shimmer.

Northern Pike *Esox lucius*

HABITAT AND RANGE: This species is extremely widespread and is found around the world in the northern hemisphere in temperate through subarctic regions. In the Northern Appalachian region, it has been widely introduced, but its native range is primarily from Pennsylvania northward through New England. It is found in many river systems and most of the large reservoirs of the Northeast. Many of these initial introductions have led to naturally reproducing populations. A limiting factor for large northern pike is sufficient cool water environments during the warm summer months. Although they prefer lake environments, northern pike may be found in some Northern Appalachian rivers, especially if they have access to large backwaters, connected swamps, or impounded areas for springtime spawning and thermal refuge during the summer.

DESCRIPTION AND NOTES: Northern pike are characterized by elongated bodies; dorsal and anal fins near the tail; cream-colored, horizontally aligned, bean-like spots on a dark body; an ambush feeding approach; and the need for cool water environments. They can reach lengths of more than forty-eight inches and forty pounds. However, a typical adult will range from twenty-four to thirty-six inches and four to ten pounds. Small, juvenile pike, less than twenty inches in length, are nicknamed "hammer handles," while very large pike over forty inches are often referred to as "gators" by some anglers. Northern pike, called "northerns" or "pike" for short, are also colloquially known as the "water wolf" due to their reputation as an apex predator in many aquatic systems. They are known to attack smaller fish being reeled in by unsuspecting anglers often at boatside, creating a splash and commotion and adding to their legend of ferocity. Northern pike are an important part of the ice fishing tradition in northeastern states. Their many nicknames are a testament to their widespread distribution, popularity, and place in angling folklore.

— *Andrew C. Gottlieb*

Cento for Northern Pike

Evening. The reservoir rimmed with tattered
rain-pocked cliffs,
                    the muted sound of rocks
colliding underwater.

Where fog trails and mist creeps,
 even as the bait fish gather, small
as tears,
   dipping down to little creeks,
a great dark thing refusing to be ignored
   the size of the fish whose head sprang
from the slush-filled abyss,
  moving huge through that darkness,
Silent.
Maybe there's still a language enough of us can speak
silence wants to be sound
Through the night your mouth has begun to open
To hunt and to have and to hold
          one strong limb below
How the next thing happens is forgotten in a blink—
    a yard of teeth.
In their hunger for red, they have eaten
    heat like butter.
Nothing stirs but the clarity of breezes
your voice released into the night
And slight, pink bones.

Tessellated Darter *Etheostoma olmstedi*

HABITAT AND RANGE: The tessellated darter occurs in warm water streams and rivers draining to the Atlantic Ocean from northern Florida to the St. Lawrence River in Ontario and Quebec. It is not found in Maine, but very strong populations exist in the Delaware, Potomac, and Susquehanna River systems.

DESCRIPTION AND NOTES: This small, riverine darter reaches two to three inches in length and has a light tan or golden/olive back and a cream-colored belly. They have distinctive, dark W- or M-shaped markings arranged along their lateral line from behind the head to the base of the tail. The "tessellated" portion of their name describes the way these markings fit together in a repeating pattern. Tessellated darters are a bottom dwelling fish, and the name "darter" refers to the way they swim by darting or scooting along in short spurts. They lack a swim bladder and like other darters have a downward sloping head. These hydrodynamic adaptations help them use water currents to stay near the bottom and move quickly while foraging or escaping predators. They prefer slow or sluggish currents and soft substrates of sand, gravel, or mud. Tessellated darters are important as a fish host species for the federally endangered dwarf wedge mussel whose parasitic larvae attach to its gills to hitch a ride to appropriate colonization habitats. They consume aquatic insect larvae such as mayflies and caddisflies, as well as larvae of the nuisance black fly. They are forage for many other bottom dwelling fishes and crayfish and are short lived, rarely exceeding four years of age.

— *Christina Seymour*

Except as Bait

> Tessellated darters have no recreational or commercial value, except as bait for larger species.
> —The Chesapeake Bay Program

Darters are *sprightly* like shy children
and the glittery rubber worms I chose
at the woodshed, holding each to the light
like selecting sequined earrings—the clip-ons

that I wore for dress-up in the photo of me
and what the adults said: *that can't be you!*
In purple boots too-big, I hooked a minnow
through its eye, without meaning to,

to catch a "rainbow fish" that slices
a serrated horizon on dad's palm.
On the way back to the Buick, my flimsy rod
and foam bucket drag along brush;

Dad says not to look at the carcass
of a housecat buzzing with green flies
like angels over a tent city—
the story of rot, the skin

that draws prey, as darters do, jerking
along the caverns of a riverbed
where their bodies marked with X or Y
disappear in stacks of striped stones,

and their short snouts search
for mosquitos, full of mammals' blood—
maybe our blood—knowing to favor the dark,
away from heron,

turtle, and kingfisher. Darters belong
to this place of *away*, to a whole body
of camouflage, by nature or by nurture,
to shadows, not knowing why.

VII — Invertebrates

HABITAT AND RANGE: This beetle is found in forests, the edges of fields, and other moist, open habitats throughout eastern North America.

DESCRIPTION AND NOTES: From spring through autumn, American carrion beetles are a common sight on animal carcasses. Their scientific name, *Necrophila* (death loving), indicates this habitat preference. In Northern Appalachia, there is one generation per year, and the adult beetles emerge from hibernation in May. Adults are oval, with a "pronotum"—(the first, shield-like thoracic segment, directly behind the head on the backs of beetles)—that is yellow with a black spot in the center. The wing covers (elytra) are black with a ridged, wrinkled pattern and are yellow tipped. Adults are about the size of a large bumble bee, and with their size, coloration, and flight patterns, they resemble bumble bees when in flight. Active during the daytime, adult American carrion beetles feed on maggots and other insect larvae that have colonized dead animals in the earlier stages of decomposition. Adults also feed on fungi and rotting plant material. American carrion beetle adults lay their eggs in animals that are in the later, drier stages of decomposition, and the larvae feed on the carrion jerky. Larvae emerge from late May to mid-July, and they resemble jet black and teardrop-shaped "roly-polys," also known as sowbugs (Isopods). When ready to pupate, the beetle larvae crawl into excavated cells in nearby soil. The life cycle from egg to adult takes approximately ten to twelve weeks. For their role in nutrient cycling, decomposers such as the American carrion beetle are a crucial component of healthy ecosystems. These beetles are also a key insect species used in forensic entomology due to the consistent timing of their feeding and egg-laying behaviors.

— *Diane LeBlanc*

Carrion Beetles

live for the sweet spot
between death and decay
                    muscle and leather

for the smell of the dead
possum/raccoon/deer/rabbit
                    to bring them into

the mating feast
the release of eggs
                    the body occupied

until flies swarm
and leave their own eggs
                    the whole mess

soon humming with maggots
and cleaned to sinew and bone
                    beetles now gone

while their larvae—armored
and hungry—devour
                    remains of remains

essential decomposers
because carrion will hoard
                    what the living need

carbon and nitrogen
to restore soil and air
                    unless a catalyst

all jaw and palp
and hammer-winged instinct
                    insists *gone, let go*

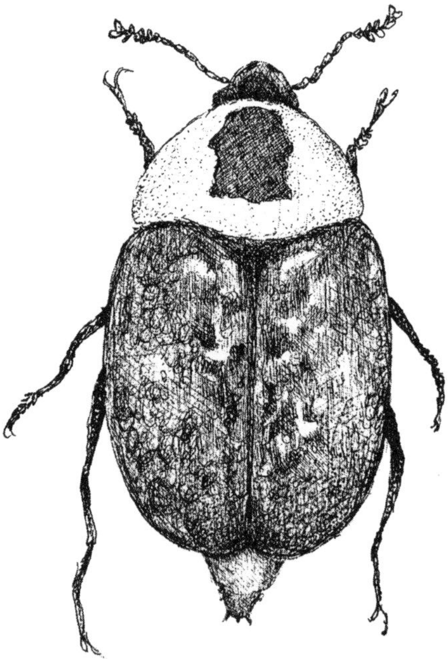

Appalachian Brook Crayfish *Cambarus bartonii*

HABITAT AND RANGE: This species of crayfish is found in cool, fast-flowing, small- to medium-sized streams, shallow ponds and lakes, springs, and wetlands throughout eastern North America.

DESCRIPTION AND NOTES: Crayfish are freshwater crustaceans that are closely related to and most resemble miniature lobsters. Crayfish occur in all varieties of freshwater habitats: groundwater seeps, streams, rivers, and wet meadows. Crayfish are omnivores, feeding on smaller invertebrates, plant material such as algae, animal waste, and various other forms of detritus. The Appalachian brook crayfish is a small- to medium-sized (one and a half to two inches long) orange-brown crayfish. This species can live for up to four years and breeds in late summer to early autumn. You may find a female crayfish carrying fertilized eggs on the underside of her tail, using thin leglike appendages called pleopods. Females carrying eggs are said to be "in berry," as the egg clusters resemble berries. The Appalachian brook crayfish is a tertiary burrower. Crayfish that are tertiary burrowers live primarily in rivers or creeks, and they create shallow burrows only during their breeding season or to escape drought or predators. Primary burrowers live in habitats near groundwater, and they excavate complex, highly developed systems of chambers, tunnels, and shafts that can be nine to ten feet deep. Raised chimneys built from excavated earth mark the entrances to these burrows. Tertiary burrowers like Appalachian brook crayfish occupy habitats near headwater streams, and their burrows are not as deep or complex as those of primary burrowers. Unlike many crayfish species, the Appalachian brook crayfish is abundant and common within its very large range. This, and the regional differences that have been observed in the species, suggest that *Cambarus bartonii* actually may be several different, endemic species in the Appalachians. Crayfish have the highest rate of endemicity of any North American animal group. Also, crayfish are vulnerable to anthropogenic actions that result in the introduction of invasive species or habitat loss or fragmentation. For these reasons, native crayfish are one of the most imperiled animal groups in the Appalachians.

— *Noah Davis*

In Berry

High on the mountain

        where the creek is almost too small for water

inches-tall chimneys line the bank.

Smokestacks never meant for smoke

carved by the claws of those who huddle within.

Their undersides pearled with eggs

tight as bubbles below a rapid

thick as nettles in July.

They bury themselves here while in berry.

The lip of the chimney a kiss above water.

The color of the sky reaching down the mud throat

to the antenna reaching up.

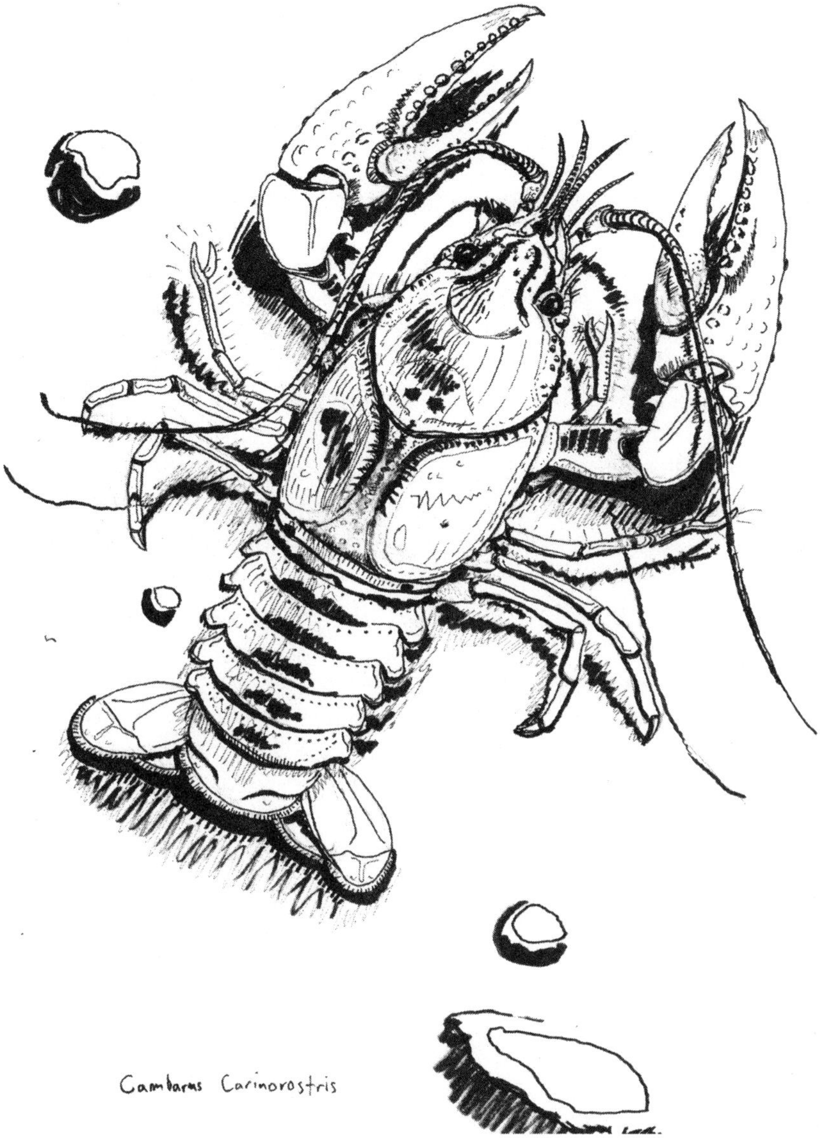

Cambarus Carinorostris

HABITAT AND RANGE: East of the Rocky Mountains, the cecropia moth is found in meadows and other open areas that are bordered by wood lots or extensive forests.

DESCRIPTION AND NOTES: Giant silkmoths (family Saturniidae) include the iconic luna moth, the regal or royal walnut moth (whose striking larvae are called hickory horned devils), and this, the cecropia moth (*Hyalophora cecropia*). Giant silkmoths are so named for their large size and for the thick, silken cocoons spun by the larvae before they pupate. *Hyalophora* species are large and colorful, and the cecropia moth is the largest *Hyalophora* and the largest moth in North America, with a wingspan of about the size of a dinner plate (five to seven inches). Adult cecropia moths have wings with bold, complex patterns in red, brown, grey, and white. Coloration and patterns can vary geographically, and cecropia moths will hybridize with other *Hyalophora* species where their ranges overlap. In the Northern Appalachians of upstate New York and New England, the large and vibrant cecropia moth is known to breed with the smaller and drabber Columbia silkmoth (*H. columbia*). When they hatch, cecropia moth larvae are black bodied and bristly, and as they grow, they turn orange bodied with black bristles. Larvae are generalists, eating leaves from dozens of different species of deciduous trees and shrubs. Before they pupate, the large larvae are seafoam green with black-spined red-orange, yellow, and pale blue knobs all along their bodies. Cecropia moths overwinter in their cocoons, which resemble large seed pods (like those of milkweeds) attached lengthwise to twigs. In Northern Appalachia, look for the purse-shaped cocoons on bare twigs between October and April, for the adults around lights at night near wooded edges between March and July, and for the larvae on maples, cherries, and other trees and woody shrubs between May and October.

— *Rebecca Foust*

Imago

On the porch tonight, a large shadow flutter-flops, then spreads itself flat on the screen:
a cecropia moth, larger & less graceful than its silkworm sister, the Luna,

a more sturdy beauty dressed in dun like a pilgrim. A child's paper-bag kite painted brown,
tan, & white, with slashes of scarlet & six eyespots that cannot see

but may be its main defense against predators. I can tell she's a female by her wingspan
broader than my hand, & by her antennae, black feather

boas longer & sparser than on the male YouTube is showing me now, after having blown
my mind with the caterpillar instars—a fever dream in black fur, chartreuse,

& aquamarine, improbably adorned with rows of tubercles, bumps bright as M & Ms.
Everything about this creature seems miraculous & rare.

Like the poignant brevity of her apogee stage, or the exquisite calibration of receptors
making her an important indicator species,

or the seven distinct states of being: beginning as one of a hundred tan beads hatched
in June, then emerging as four instars, each an eating machine

more swollen & neon, then within the cocoon, the pupa in winter swoon, a lacquered
scarab in whose last molt occurs ecdysis of the entire digestive tract,

even the proboscis other moths use to sip the tears of sleeping birds. Finally, the imago
emerges, a worm with head & wing bumps that, as I watch at 5× speed,

are pumped full of fluid to rise, unfurl, & swell until she is all pheromone cistern, scent
receptor & wing. For two weeks she will survive

on what she's herself made & stored, able to fly & cast a scent plume I can interpret
as a kind of longing. An epitome of singularity of purpose

& teleological fulfillment, living till she meets her mate, who will find her by her scent
& whom she will in turn assess by divination of *his* pheromones.

These things are miracle enough, but what fills me with awe is what she must endure
to enact her transformation—six times she must rupture herself

to give birth to herself—six times, shed all she was & is. First, the egg's blind & safe world
shattered into cacophony heat & light,

then each molt's long shuddered sine waves of agon as she labors to crawl out of her skin,
the goggled head rooting for light, the clear case falling away,

one tarsal then the next groping, dragging the body through what has by now become
redundant—her past—but not entirely, because she does not turn away,

she turns around to face it, then eats it whole. She's new, but a new that accepts
& subsumes all she was. Imagine that moment before emergence,

reckoning with loss of everything she is & was, & the moment after, when she looks back
like Lot's wife to survey what's been left, but then—unlike Lot's wife—accepts it,

literally merging present with past to form her future. I like to think not that the imago
feels no hunger, but that she feels hunger that is its own fulfillment,

a hunger that needs no mouth. Which I cannot help but liken to spirit, to longing for God,
who made us but made us without the means to take him in.

Or maybe, it's hunger refined into the kind that seeks to connect us to kind. Looking at
the moth on my porch screen, whose slow breathing of wings

seems so pacific, I think again of those terrible throes on the brink of what cannot seem
possible—the destruction of everything—

to incarnate freedom & negation of need, as close to pure energy as a body can be.
Embodied finally as flight, & twitch of tip

of antenna while she waits for the mate she will choose. In this imago, an image of what
we might aspire to achieve: an ecstasy of relief

from the need to provide, in a form that carries & knits the strand of all we are & were.
Maybe in fact this moth's highest purpose is not bodily satiation

or love, or procreation, but full expression of being: replete, finally complete—for one
brief span exhilarate—flying all night, navigating by moonlight.

HABITAT AND RANGE: The common eastern firefly is found in woodland borders, fields, lawns, and other habitats throughout the eastern United States.

DESCRIPTION AND NOTES: Few sights in the Northern Appalachians are more magical than the flashes of thousands of fireflies on a summer evening. Here, these fireflies, or "lightning bugs," are likely to be common eastern fireflies, which is the most common firefly in the eastern United States. Fireflies are not "flies" or "bugs" but soft-bodied beetles, and they use different flash patterns to communicate warnings to predators and displays for potential mates—or prey. The females of some species mimic the flashes of other firefly species to lure males to their untimely ends. Often identified as *Photinus pyralis,* the name common eastern firefly actually refers to a group of three physically identical species, called the *Photinus pyralis* group. These three species—*P. pyralis, P. australis,* and *P. scintillans*—are impossible to identify using morphological characteristics alone, but they *are* distinct behaviorally and geographically and thus can be identified correctly when they are alive and in their natural habitat. At dusk in late June and July in the Northern Appalachians, look in open fields for a low-flying firefly that flashes and dips, making a long, yellow, lazy J-shaped pattern in the air. That is *Photinus pyralis,* the most common of the three species in the common eastern firefly species group. In Pennsylvania, where a firefly is the state insect, the small town of Tionesta holds a firefly festival every June. Here, the dazzling displays of a different species, the synchronous firefly (*P. carolinus*) are so popular that registration for the free festival is by lottery only.

— *Aimee Nezhukumatathil*

Firefly Nocturne

I never feared the dark. I welcomed it, let it rush
into my unbuttoned blouse. When I was a girl,
I learned the light of a firefly signals *summer.*
Signals *heart. Bare skin.* There is a certain sparkle
of beetles that knows how to blink in synchronicity—
a visual heartbeat in the darkest owl-filled atria
of a forest. Once, we held our own universe
in the morning rain. And like the firefly, I've mistaken
too many cars too many street and porch lights
for small moons. In late spring, the first branchlets

of bee balm and calendula color the air. Eventually peeping frogs shiver awake when it turns warm again. When we are old, I hope the firefly conversation we have still thumps and thumps. I hope it's still green-gold.

Eastern Elliptio Mussel *Elliptio complanata*

HABITAT AND RANGE: Eastern elliptio mussels are found in ponds, creeks, lakes, and rivers throughout the eastern United States.

DESCRIPTION AND NOTES: There are 890 known species of freshwater mussels worldwide; one-third of these species are found in the United States. Freshwater mussels can be as small as a black bean and as large as a cake pan. They are important culturally to Native Americans as resources used for food, tools, and jewelry. They are important ecologically for their ability to filter contaminants, bacteria, and algae from water and for their vital roles in food webs. Common names of freshwater mussels can be comical, such as wartyback, monkeyface, or pigtoe. Some freshwater mussels can live for one hundred years. The life cycle of a freshwater mussel is complex and fascinating. Larval mussels, called glochidia, require fish or amphibian hosts to complete the freshwater mussel life cycle. Adult mussels use various strategies to attract potential hosts for their larvae. These strategies can include using their own tissue as lures that resemble worms or small fishes to attract larger fish hosts. When a fish or amphibian comes within range of the adult mussels the glochidia are released and attach to the gills of their hosts. After a period ranging from one week to an entire winter, the glochidia mature into juvenile mussels that resemble miniature adults, and they detach from their hosts to finish out their lives in the substrate. The eastern elliptio mussel is oval or trapezoidal in shape and can grow to nearly four inches in length. This is one of the most abundant and long-lived freshwater mussels in the eastern United States. It can be found in a variety of substrates (silt, sand, pebble), in a variety of lotic (flowing) and lentic (still) waters, and its average life span is twenty years. This mussel can use several fish species as hosts for their glochidia, but the best host fish for the eastern elliptio is the endangered American eel (*Anguilla rostrata*). American eels are the only freshwater species of eel in North America, and they have an equally complex life cycle. Young American eels migrate thousands of miles from their birthplace in the Sargasso Sea to inland streams and rivers, where they can live for decades before journeying back to the sea to breed. Factors such as overfishing and habitat fragmentation from dams have decimated its populations. Because of the relationship between fish and mussel, dam removal and other conservation efforts that benefit the American eel also benefit the eastern elliptio mussel.

— *Anni Liu*

Bivalve Means My Body Is a Muscle Made for Clapping

Down here in the substrate, crooked in the clay
we eke out a murky subsistence of suck and spit.

A brown and yellowish commoner
among commoners, we're thought of, if we are

thought of at all, as headless bottom-feeders
buried in a sullied bed, indiscriminately

mouthing whatever drifts our way. I hear
it isn't respectable to feed on particulates,

to comb through the nameless, discarded bits
not meant to sustain a life. And yet

we proliferate in abundance. Indiscriminate,
it may seem, but our gills appraise

all that has been surrendered to the current,
and tasting it, learn to praise the water's amplitude,

our bottomless commitment to the glut of multiplicity.
See, it's all in the filtering—the wisdom gleaned

from having swallowed the river's entire length
to know what should and should not be kept.

It is in this that we become abundant,
resplendent, clamping down with our single foot

our portion of silt and spill. Elliptical,
unnoticed, we dig into this mud, releasing

what doesn't sustain us. The result is a clarity
you fetishize and mistake for purity, but purity

holds no water for us. We enfold a gleaming interiority.
In the bedrock, we flex an endless unfolding.

Miner Bee *Andrena* spp.

HABITAT AND RANGE: Miner bees are found nearly worldwide, except for Australia and South America. The majority of known miner or mining bees are located in the northern hemisphere, occupying a very wide variety of habitats, including fields and forests.

DESCRIPTION AND NOTES: As of January 2023, there are 3,594 known species of bees in the United States and 461 (12.8 percent) of these are *Andrena* bees. *Andrena* bees, commonly called miner or mining bees, are known for their tolerance to cold, and they inhabit many environments that differ in altitude, temperature, hydrology, precipitation, and pollen sources. The color of *Andrena* bees varies from drab grey or brown to red or metallic blue, and their sizes range from that of the tiniest fruit fly to the size of a large bumble bee. Female *Andrena* are recognizable by the hairy grooves (facial fovea) that line the inner margins of their eyes. The size and shape of the facial fovea and the color of their hairs can be unique among species. All *Andrena* are ground nesters. Some populations aggregate their nests into something of a neighborhood, and these neighborhoods may endure for decades, outlasting dozens of generations of bees. Some *Andrena* bees visit a wide variety of plants, but many are specialists. These choosy bees are oligolectic in that the pollen that they collect is from only a related group of plants (e.g., huckleberries and blueberries) or from a single type of plant (e.g., willows). The spring beauty miner bee (*A. erigeniae*) is a common, early spring bee of the eastern woodlands. This species is an oligolege of spring beauty flowers (*Claytonia virginica*), and you will see the hind legs of the tiny females clothed in the plant's pink pollen. Also in the spring, watch for the large trout lily miner bees (*A. erythronii*) buzzing through eastern forests, searching for trout lilies (*Erythronium*). Later in the spring and into midsummer, you may find the metallic blue waterleaf miner bee (*A. geraniii*) on its host plant, the waterleafs (*Hydrophyllum*). In northern hardwood forests, the fragile miner bee (*A. fragilis*) visits its favorite dogwoods. If you are near bogs, fens, and wet meadows in the late summer, and especially in Vermont, you may be very lucky to see a Parnassus miner bee (*A. parnassiae*) on a grass of the Parnassus flower. And as the leaves are starting to turn in the Northern Appalachians, the hairy-banded miner bee (*A. hirticincta*), a medium-sized bee with lemon-yellow hairs, is commonly seen among the goldenrods.

— Stacie Cassarino

The Miner Bee

It is strenuous work. She must do it alone.
Can you hear her humming, the solitary mother under-
ground who knows her place, hollowing the earth
into tunnels: in orchards dry with the scent
of apples, burrowing hedgerows and quarries,
on sloping hillsides and ditch-cuts,
nesting in road verges and coastal dunes at dawn,
through blueberry fields at the forest's edge,
or where children play soccer, kicking
the sing-song sun of afternoon.
She hurtles forward and back on transparent wings.
She is fast. A flash of flight, though no fight
for marauding males, zigzagging
to catch the mother mid-air and tumble her to the ground.

Can you see the flare of her blood-orange thorax,
a gentle mother doing her duty, *all hard shell, soft core,*
without a colony. *The life of a single mother.*
The difficult life. Why is her tale narrated
as hardship? *Life is tough for the miner.*
Why crown her heroic for doing it all herself?
She peers big-eyed at the world above her,
fertile architect, faithful pollinator, noisemaker.
Alighting on a bloom of goldenrods,
drawn to the twilight of evening primroses,
she gathers pollen with her mouth, a load half her body weight.
And who depends on whom?
Is it the aster who needs the mother
to be the diligent courier, or the mother rewarded
by the flower's nectar, a source of life?
Is it the mother who needs her young,
or do they, in blossom,
need their own wild release?
Spring for emergence. Spring for the earth animated,
for the music we walk all over simply
moving from here to there
holding our hearts on the outside enflamed, oblivious
to the beauty of their buzzing bodies coming awake.

Monarch Butterfly *Danaus plexippus plexippus*

HABITAT AND RANGE: Monarch butterflies are found in open habitats (fields, meadows, roadsides) of North America, central America, and northern South America.

DESCRIPTION AND NOTES: The monarch butterfly is perhaps the most famous butterfly in North America, both for its bold colors and also for its epic migrations. Monarch larvae grow to a mature length of two inches with alternating bands of black, yellow, and white stripes and with a pair of long black filaments at each end. Larvae feed on milkweeds (genus *Asclepias*), which contain cardiac glycosides that make them distasteful for most birds and mammals. Despite this, monarch larvae are still susceptible to parasitism by flies and tiny wasps and also predation by various other invertebrates such as spiders, predatory stink bugs, and mantids. After fifteen to twenty days in the larval stage, monarch caterpillars crawl to a safe location away from the host plant, hang upside down from a spun silken anchor, and begin to pupate. Like the larvae and the adults, the gold-dotted, sea green monarch pupae are easily recognizable. Adult monarchs emerge from their pupae after approximately two weeks. Adult monarchs have bright orange wings striped with black and dotted with white along the outer edges, and their average wingspan is three and a half inches. Adult males can be distinguished from females by the single black spot ("scent scale") on the center vein of each hindwing. The migratory monarch butterfly (*Danaus plexippus plexippus*) is a subspecies of monarch that is famous for its epic journeys across the Americas, migrating to and from overwintering sites in California and Mexico. In 2022, due to losses of winter habitat and observed declines in western and eastern populations of migratory monarchs, the status of this subspecies was changed to Endangered by the International Union for Conservation of Nature (IUCN) for its Red List of Threatened Species. In Northern Appalachia, look for northbound migrating monarch adults searching for nectar plants and milkweeds in the spring. In this region, there are two to four broods of larvae per year. From spring to autumn, look for larvae on milkweeds and adults on milkweeds and other nectar plants. In September and October, look for flocks of adults beginning their long journeys southward. A subspecies of the viceroy butterfly (*Limenitis archippus archippus*), a distantly related monarch mimic, is also native to this region. The adults are similar to monarchs but have a smaller average wingspan (two and three-quarters inches) and an additional thick black line across the width of each hindwing. Viceroy larvae resemble brown and white bird droppings and feed primarily on willows and poplars.

— Sean Prentiss

To Flutter

We throw our hands to air, cascading
milkweed kites into November's
slate gray sky—Little Girl and me,
this middle-aged dad who lives
with older father worry. Will these
seeds find soil? Will these monarchs
—color of dawn's orange sunrise
and trimmed in funeral's black
and white lace—reach overwintering
Mexican fir forests? Will there be
enough descendants for monarchs
to return in fifty years? Will I live
long enough to cry at Little Girl's wedding,

to cradle her newborns? I shake away
these thoughts, let them flutter elsewhere,
as Little Girl and I watch the breeze float
pappus and seed wherever it will, just as
our summer breezes bluster our monarchs
to and fro, just as life will float Little Girl
and me wherever it will. She and I,
we smile completely separate smiles as
she gazes at swaying seeds in flight and says,
The seeds look like butterflies. And they do.
They do as they drift, soar and ripple. If only
I could learn to sail this world as lightly
as a milkweed seed, as a flittering monarch,
as the mind of a child. To flutter so gently
upon life's many tumultuous breezes.

VIII — Fungi

HABITAT AND RANGE: Common in the United States and eastern Canada, this fungi is found from late June to September on soil within deciduous forests or in mixed stands of hardwoods and conifers; it is particularly associated with oaks. This tree symbiont occurs singly or in groups and can be found in the same area for years.

DESCRIPTION AND NOTES: Around three inches tall, this egg-yolk yellow mushroom is a favorite of gourmet chefs. The cap is one-half to five inches wide; its shape is convex with an in-rolled margin. With age, the cap center may become slightly sunken or funnel shaped, and the margin gets wavy, lobed, and irregular. Under the cap are folds resembling gills but with blunt, rounded edges. These forking and cross-veined folds descend the stalk, which is yellowish white and from three-quarters to three inches tall. Chanterelles have a unique odor, similar to an apricot. All chanterelle species are edible. But there are poisonous, look-alike species. For example, the poisonous jack-o'-lantern mushroom (*Omphalotus olearius*) has true gills and grows on wood. Before you eat any mushroom species for the first time, you must have your identification confirmed by an experienced collector and consumer of edible, wild mushrooms. Like the morel and many other fungal species, the chanterelles are mycorrhizal—existing underground as a network of cells, collectively a mycelium, connected to fine tree roots. This subterranean transportation system helps tree roots absorb water and nutrients, in turn the tree shares nutrients and carbohydrates with the symbiotic fungus.

— *Alison Hawthorne Deming*

American Golden Chanterelle

I have picked them mostly in Canada.
They don't care about borders
except the one that marks
the underneath from the air.

Most of their lives are a tangle
of threads felting the dark soil
under forests and when they rise
oh it is a golden morning so loud,

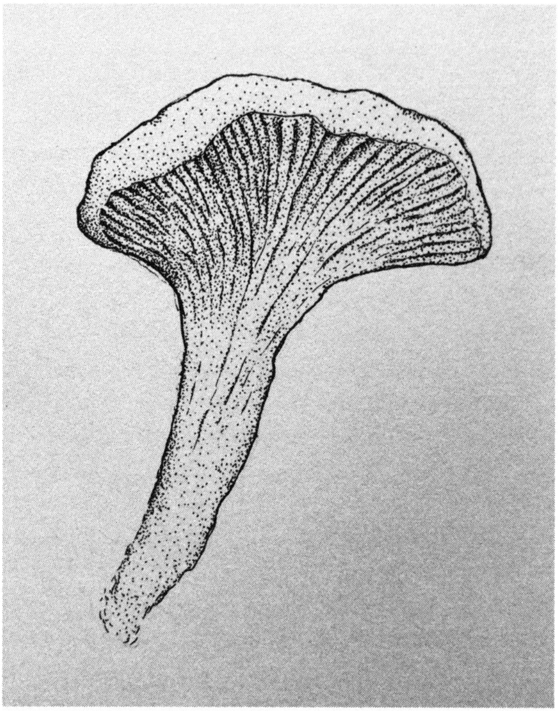

immodest, brash, like horn players
on Mardi Gras. But why do I think
of cities when I see them? Yellow
lights of tiny skyscrapers shining in the dark.

I walk along a cliff where spruce
and balsam fir look down on me.
They have stood so long in place
I am a mere itch on their landscape.

But the chanterelles know me
their fruiting bodies so quick and gone
while under Earth's cover
the mycelial rave rolls on.

HABITAT AND RANGE: Chicken of the woods is common in forests throughout Northern Appalachia and beyond on logs, stumps, and shallow roots of living, dying, and dead deciduous trees. The "chicken" is typically associated with older oaks, poplar, maple, cherry, and birch.

DESCRIPTION AND NOTES: This edible polypore, also called sulfur shelf, can be both a wood decayer and a tree parasite causing heart rot. Look for this species from May to October. When suddenly you spot an unusual splash of yellow and orange in the distant forest understory, you are likely looking at the brightly colored chicken of the woods. This fungus is composed of multiple, fan-shaped, overlapping shelves, each of which are from two and a half to twelve inches wide and one-half to one inch thick. Shelf tops are bright orange with an orange or yellowish wavy or lobed margin. Pores underneath each shelf are bright sulfur yellow. It is not unusual to find a clump of shelves as large as a soccer ball. Some logs and stumps have multiple fungal clumps of varying sizes. The growth of shelf polypores is at the edge of the fan or cap. This is the softest and arguably the best tasting and least stringy part of the chicken mushroom. Older specimens are dry, chewy, and tough. Because this polypore is an annual, its visible fruiting body slowly bleaches white and decays over the year. With a hint of citrus when cooked, this species can be a meat substitute for chicken or lobster. It can be fried, sautéed, baked, or used in a soup; there are hundreds of recipes for this fungal species. Fresh specimens preserve well if kept refrigerated for a few days. The showy chicken of the woods is a very different looking species when compared with the dull-brown hen of the woods fungus (*Grifola frondose*) which is also edible.

— *Eleanor Stanford*

Chicken of the Woods

Death arrives in its orange skirts.
Flame-bright flounce, lighter
toward the edges. The visible
aspect—the part you carry
home, sauté with onions, post
a picture of on Instagram—that's only
the fruiting body. Opportunistic,
this chicken, plucking its chutzpah
from the wounds of trees. What

embrittlement. What game of nerve.
Fowl play. Sometimes death
gives the appearance of being
terrestrial.

Crown-tipped Coral *Artomyces pyxidatus*

HABITAT AND RANGE: During spring, summer, and fall, this wood-decay (saprobe) fungus is found singly or scattered on decaying trees, stumps, and fallen limbs of willow, aspen, yellow poplar, maple, birch, and other hardwoods. This species is found throughout North America; it is more common east of the Rocky Mountains.

DESCRIPTION AND NOTES: There are numerous species of coral fungi, all characterized by fruiting bodies with upright branches. Many are difficult to identify. The crown-tipped coral is relatively unique because it is one of a few coral species found only on decaying wood. This coral species is white or pale yellow with multiple branches; it has the appearance of a miniature candelabrum. Collectively the branches of a single specimen are up to five inches tall, one and a half to four inches wide, and each branch is slightly expanded at the end and tipped with two to six points giving it the appearance of a crown. Spores (the fungal analog of seeds) develop on the branches of this fruiting body, whereas on other fungal species, spores develop on gills, folds, and teeth or in pores and puffballs. Similar to ocean corals, terrestrial corals are very photogenic. Photos of fungi are useful for art, fungi identification, and authenticating the location of a potentially rare or unusual species. Photographing fungi and trying to identify your image can be fun and may be the first step in becoming a fungi aficionado or budding mycologist (a person who studies fungi). If you find a crown-tipped coral on a particular log one year, it is likely you will find it on the same log in succeeding years given the timing of favorable, usually damp, weather.

— *Adam Giannelli*

Crown-tipped Coral

You come blessed with two metaphors:

a series of branches that resemble an ocean coral,

and the little crowns at the tip

of each branch, anointing them. What more can I add?

You're a choir harmonizing in white shirts,

a castle with many turrets, a class

in which all the students have raised their hands.

When I look at you, I don't know *is* from *are*.
Even the mycelium from which you grow
is branched. I walk over matted leaves through
the forest, dim as the sea floor, examining
shady spots and fallen trees.
The field guide warns us not to confuse you
with lookalikes, which grow
on the ground. Sprouting from an old log,
your pearly canopy resembles the forest itself,
and you break down wood so the forest
can grow. Through this cycle, your branches never end.
You can be fried with butter and garlic, crackling,
and your aroma wafts through the kitchen
as you wilt, browning, in the pan, and we place you
over rye toast. "Earthy," says Mary.
"I've been missing out," says Tommy.
Around the table, we pass wine and tell stories.
Like the arms of the candelabrum
in the center, each of us holds a flame. Lifting a fork
I break you down, but what will I give back
now that we all wear crowns?

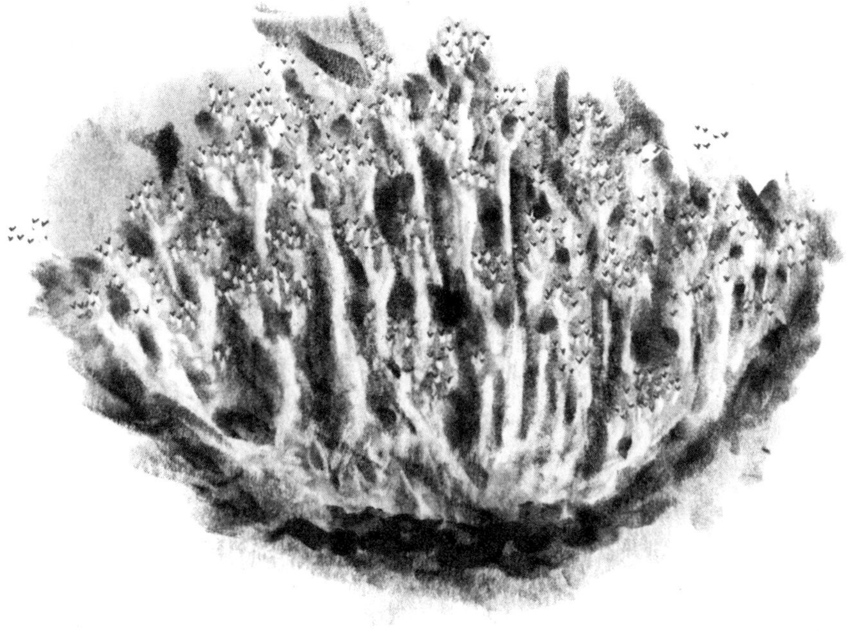

HABITAT AND RANGE: Common in North America east of the Great Plains, this large saprophore decomposes grass, leaves, and other organic litter. It can be found growing from the ground singly and in clusters or fairy rings in open, deciduous woodlots, lawns, meadows, fields, grassy ditches, and disturbed areas.

DESCRIPTION AND NOTES: *Calvatia gigantea* is a big white ball or oblong blob; it is often compared in size to a softball or volleyball. While usually between eight and twenty inches in diameter, *C. gigantea* can exceed three feet wide, and a fifty-pound specimen is on record. A short, thick stalk attaches the puffball to the ground. This saprobe may fruit in the same vicinity for years. Fruiting occurs from July through October. The giant puffball is edible; a prime specimen will be six inches or larger in diameter and totally white inside. The inside of an older specimen will be discolored yellowish or greenish brown as a result of spore development, indicating it is no longer a choice edible. Puffballs do not preserve well. A better alternative is to leave the growing puffball in place and only cut off what you can eat within a day or two. The puffball, preserved in place, will continue to grow, and you may be able to harvest a few more meals from it before it discolors and eventually sporulates. Giant puffballs are prolific spore producers. An oft-repeated and calculated figure is the astounding number of spores, seven trillion, that a two-foot-long specimen of *C. gigantea* is capable of producing. For comparison, seven trillion seconds equals 221,817 years. The vast majority of these microscopic spores fall on barren surfaces and fail to germinate. But a rare few will land on a fertile surface, extend fibers called mycelia into the ground where they may intertwine with other mycelia, and eventually result in a new population of giant puffballs.

— *K. A. Hays*

How to Be *Calvatia gigantea*

Be the spore in the air.
        Be held by air, and also let free
                to roam light—you, and many like you.

Soon, you—and many like you—
        will go down to live in the dark,
                in the dirt—to be held,

and to be let open—
        so you-the-one seeps into
                you-the-many.

A host of you will lace the dirt. Wait
without waiting, as strings
in the dark—you won't wish

for warmth, for wet—you'll sleep,
and in your sleep, you'll wish without wishing,
and soon the wet and warmth

will wake you. You-the-many will be glad.
Make of the many
a fruit to touch the air—a sphere

to swell, great and thick—
be a sphere that glows in the grass
like a moon, like a child's lost ball,

odd beauty, crater and crack—
you, large and round as a laugh,
you, tiny strings in the soil—

and then you'll be dust inside the ball.
Like a breath, you'll be held in, and then
be blown out—to wander.

In gladness to wander and fall.
In a dark-bright wind,
a cloud of you will drift again.

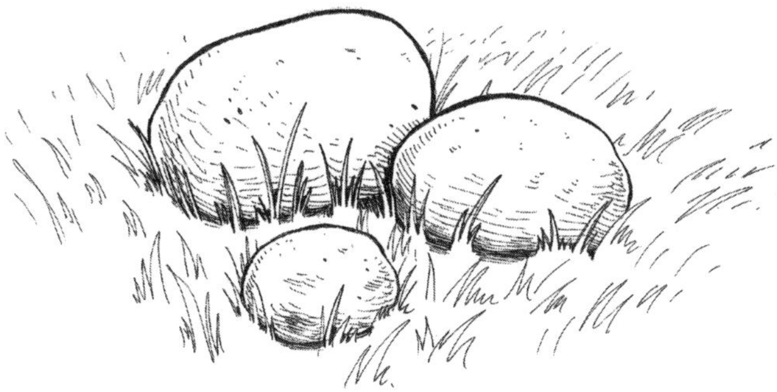

Scarlet Elf Cup *Sarcoscypha austriaca*

HABITAT AND RANGE: Found in Europe and in North America east of the Rocky Mountains, scarlet elf cup is common and widespread in the deciduous forests of Northern Appalachia. This saprobe prefers damp habitats where it feeds on dead and decaying organic matter. Look for them on fallen hardwood branches and on rotting, moss-covered wood, some of which may be buried in litter.

DESCRIPTION AND NOTES: When not covered by fallen leaves, this easy-to-spot, bright red disk is approximately one to two inches across with a flat center and upturned edges forming a shallow cup. The cup's margin is hairless and incurved. Compared to the red interior of the cup, the exterior appears paler, sometimes orange, largely due to its being covered with a tangle of curly white hairs visible only with the aid of a hand lens or microscope. The cup's stalk is short, sometimes sessile, and may be completely hidden in moss or litter. Fruiting occurs from early to late spring. Cups occur singly or in clusters, and, if the weather is cool and damp, cups may persist for several weeks. These saprobes have a role in rotting wood, thereby releasing nutrients that help promote the growth of spring plants. Under the heading of "fun for kids," elf cups actively expel their spores into the air. You can see this by blowing across the top of the cup. The resultant quick temperature change will trigger older cups to shoot up clouds of spores visible to the naked eye. Along with snowdrops, morel mushrooms, and robins, these strikingly beautiful, small fungi are bright harbingers of spring.

— *janan alexandra*

Field Guide to the Scarlet Elf Cup

> Like animals, fungi must find something to eat.
> Yet fungal eating is often generous: it makes worlds for others.
> —Anna Lowenhaupt Tsing, "The Mushroom at the End of the World"

Initially spherical, the fruit bodies
of this winter mushroom curl

to form a shallow saucer,
rim puckered just enough

to hold the wet red interior.
I see: mouths upturned

in the leaflitter, throats open
& waiting for rain.

A welcome sight from winter's
glass edge, the mossy cups

arrive in clusters of three & four,
pulling springtime

from the snow-starred
annals of February.

Heads tilted skyward
they are earnest as children.

If you lower yours to theirs,
you might catch the *pouff!* of breath:

a cloud of spores released
along the woodland floor

like fairy dust, which it is—
food for the rodents

& slugs, cupped palms
where the elves go to drink

& the gnats drift slowly down
to wash their wings.

Turkey Tail *Trametes versicolor*

HABITAT AND RANGE: This species is found on decaying wood of both conifer and deciduous trees. It fruits from spring through fall and persists through the winter and often for successive seasons. It is found throughout temperate forests in the northern hemisphere, and it is common in Northern Appalachia.

DESCRIPTION AND NOTES: This very attractive, potato-chip-thin, fungus has fan-shaped, overlapping one to four inches wide, stalkless caps, some fused laterally, that may cover the side of a log or appear as a rosette atop a rotting limb or stump. When fresh, the cap is flexible. The species name, *versicolor* (different colors), refers to the concentric bands of varying colors that comprise the upper surface of each cap. The outermost band—sometimes only a narrow, wavy edge—is white, ivory, or tan. Other bands may be various shades of purple, brown, tan, cinnamon, orange, grey, blue, and green. The cap's surface, consisting of microscopic hairs, feels velvety. The underside of each cap consists of very small, round, white to light yellow pores. The medicinal benefits of turkey tail mushrooms are legion. A common medicinal fungi, it has been used in traditional Chinese medicine for over two thousand years to promote health, strength, and longevity. It is credited with boosting immune systems, promoting digestion, combatting chronic fatigue, reducing inflammation, and fighting cancer. There is an entire industry that sells turkey tail fungus products. If you want to collect your own turkey tail mushrooms to make tea, you can take some comfort knowing that no turkey tail look-alike species is poisonous. Still, confirm your identification with an experienced mushroom collector. Clean off the collected caps, dry them, and chop or grind them into small pieces, the smaller the better. Put one tablespoon in a saucepan, add two cups of water, bring to a boil, and then simmer for about one hour. Next, strain and drink the tea. You can add other ingredients like turmeric, lemon essential oil (one drop), and honey.

— *M. J. Iuppa*

Turkey Tail

Fallen birch, lying obliquely on a mat
of soggy moss, hosts a resurrection:

ruffled fans of thin yet flexible
fungi, distinguished by rings of

color: white, gray, reddish-brown,
feeding upon this dead trunk's

medicinal core.
                    Velvety to the touch, *Turkey*

Tail gleams silver in sun, while
its underside reveals a mass of

small pores, exhaling
breath in winter.

It's hard to tell if this is the cure.
They say they grow everywhere,

making it impossible to be quick
in naming what one sees with

a naked eye. So, look closely
before light departs.

Yellow Morel — *Morchella americana*

HABITAT AND RANGE: Except for the hottest and coldest regions, this species is widespread in North America and common in Northern Appalachian forests. It is a mycorrhizal fungus, growing in association with the tree roots of mixed hardwoods and conifers, notably ash, elm, aspen, poplar, sycamore, oak, old apple trees, and pine. An organic litter layer atop slightly alkaline soil favors morels, as do wildfires, storms, floods, insect infestations, or anything stressing or killing trees, which for a few years may stimulate an extraordinary proliferation of morel mushrooms.

DESCRIPTION AND NOTES: The yellow morel, two to twelve inches tall, has a light tan to yellowish spongelike cap that is taller than wide and approximately shaped like an oval. The bottom of this cap is attached to a white or cream-colored stalk that is one to five inches tall and one-half to two and a half inches wide. Morels are entirely hollow from cap top to stalk bottom. The yellow morel puts in its two-week appearance between late March and early June, about the time when Mayapple plants appear and oak leaves are the size of a nickel. Mid-April to mid-May is prime morel hunting time in Northern Appalachia. Because of their taste and their spatial/temporal rarity, morels are highly sought after, and, when found, their locations are kept secret. The exterior pits and ridges of morel caps often harbor little critters, but with proper care and preparation, morels are a choice edible. However, a look-alike species, the false morel, is poisonous. For this reason and a few others, fungal novices are always encouraged to accompany an experienced morel hunter or join a mycology club to learn how to positively identify both edible and nonedible mushrooms. A well-illustrated fungal field guide is also a must for mushroom identifiers. Morels have resisted easy cultivation. This fact, their brief appearance, and their spotty distribution contributes to the recreational value of morel hunting. Fungal forays and hunting specifically for morels are, in essence, the adult equivalent of Easter egg hunts.

— *Matthew J. Spireng*

Morel

Prune of the woods, we'd call them,
old sponge, nothing we'd ever think of
eating as kids. Playing in the woods
in spring, we'd spot them near where
Father had cut a tree for firewood—

dying apple from an old orchard,
oak farther from the house—and once
near an elm that was dropping leaves
prematurely at the edge of the lawn.
One day there was nothing, the next:

there they were. We'd kick them then.
Mock them. Wrinkled mushrooms
on hollow stalks sprouting from
the ground. Aged now, I was asked
by a friend just last spring if I ever found

morels in my woods. I'd heard the name,
but didn't know them, and couldn't
tell her yes or no. She described them,
saying *sponge* at one point, and I knew.
Delicious, she said. I was hesitant, but found

several near the stump of a dying apple I'd
cut the year before and took them to her, shared
with her once she confirmed. That evening,
morels sauteed in butter in a pan, I was reminded
how foolish children can be.

Bibliography for Further Reading

Introduction

Bonta, Marcia. *Appalachian Summer.* Pittsburgh, Pa.: University of Pittsburgh Press, 1999.

Fergus, Charles, and Amelia Hansen. *Wildlife of Pennsylvania and the Northeast.* Mechanicsburg, Pa.: Stackpole Books, 2000.

Stephenson, Steven L. *A Natural History of the Central Appalachians.* Morgantown: West Virginia University Press, 2013.

Weidensaul, Scott. *Mountains of the Heart: A Natural History of the Appalachians.* Golden, Colo.: Fulcrum Publishing, 1994.

I. Trees and Shrubs

Fergus, Charles. *Trees of Pennsylvania and the Northeast.* Mechanicsburg, Pa.: Stackpole Books, 2002.

Tallamy, Douglas W. *Bringing Nature Home: How You Can Sustain Wildlife with Native Plants.* Portland, Oreg.: Timber Press, 2009.

Wessells, Tom. *Reading the Forested Landscape: A Natural History of New England.* Woodstock, Vt.: Countryman Press, 1997.

II. Wildflowers

Moerman, Daniel E. *Native American Food Plants: An Ethnobotanical Dictionary.* Portland, Oreg.: Timber Press, 2010.

Moerman, Daniel E. *Native American Medicinal Plants: An Ethnobotanical Dictionary.* Portland, Oreg.: Timber Press, 2009.

Rhoads, Anna Fowler, and Timothy A. Block. *The Plants of Pennsylvania: An Illustrated Manual.* Philadelphia: University of Pennsylvania Press, 2007.

III. Mammals

Dout, J. K., C. A. Heppenstall, and J. E. Guilday. *Mammals of Pennsylvania.* Pittsburgh: Pennsylvania Game Commission and Carnegie Institute, 1977.

Godin, Alfred. J. *Wild Mammals of New England.* Baltimore: Johns Hopkins University Press, 1977.

Steele, Michael A., Margaret C. Brittingham, Timothy J. Maret, and Joseph F. Merritt, eds. *Terrestrial Vertebrates of Pennsylvania: A Complete Guide to Species of Conservation Concern.* Baltimore: Johns Hopkins University Press, 2010.

IV. Birds

Bonta, Marcia. *Appalachian Spring.* Pittsburgh: University of Pittsburgh Press, 1991.

Cornell Laboratory of Ornithology. Online Guide to Birds and Birdwatching. https://www.allaboutbirds.org.

Sibley, David Allen. *The Sibley Field Guide to Birds of Eastern North America.* New York: Alfred A. Knopf, 2016.

V. Reptiles and Amphibians

Behler, John L., and F. Wayne King. *National Audubon Society Field Guide to North American Reptiles and Amphibians.* New York: Alfred A. Knopf, 1998.

Hulse, Arthur. C., Ellen Censky, and C. J. McCoy. *Amphibians and Reptiles of Pennsylvania and the Northeast.* Ithaca, N.Y.: Cornell University Press, 2001.

Tyning, Thomas A. *Stokes Nature Guides: A Guide to Amphibians and Reptiles.* Boston: Little Brown, 1990.

VI. Fish

Page, Lawrence. A., and Brooks M. Burr. *Peterson Field Guide to Freshwater Fishes.* Boston: Houghton Mifflin Harcourt, 2011.

Patterson, Davis A., and Matt Patterson. *Freshwater Fish of the Northeast.* Lebanon, N.H.: University Press of New England, 2010.

Stauffer, Jay R., Jr., Robert W. Criswell, and Douglas P. Fischer. *The Fishes of Pennsylvania.* El Paso, Tex.: Cichlid Press, 2016.

VII. Invertebrates

Hamrsky, Jan. *Freshwater Life: Macro Photography of Aquatic Insects and Other Freshwater invertebrates.* lifeinfreshwater.net.

Iowa State University, Department of Plant Pathology, Entomology, and Microbiology. Identification, Images, and Information for Insects, Spiders and Their Kin for the United States and Canada. bugguide.net.

Sverdrup-Thygeson, Anne. *Extraordinary Insects: The Fabulous, Indispensable Creatures Who Run Our World.* New York: Simon and Schuster, 2020.

VIII. Fungi

Boddy, Lynne, and Wenjia Tang. *Humongous Fungus: The Weird and Wonderful Kingdom of Fungi.* New York: DK Children, 2021.

Marrone, Teresa, and Walt Sturgeon. *Mushrooms of the Northeast: A Simple Guide to Common Mushrooms.* Cambridge, Minn.: Adventure Publications, 2016.

Sheldrake, Merlin. *Entangled Life: How Fungi Make Our Worlds, Change Our Minds, and Shape Our Futures.* New York: Random House, 2020.

Contributors

Poets

JANAN ALEXANDRA is a Lebanese American poet currently based in New England. Her poems have appeared in *Beloit Poetry Journal, Ninth Letter, Gulf Coast, Ploughshares, Mizna,* and elsewhere. In addition to her work as a writer and creative writing teacher, she plays the fiddle in a folk duo called Sweet May Dews.

DAVID BAKER is author of thirteen books of poetry, recently *Whale Fall* (Norton, 2022) and *Swift: New and Selected Poems* (Norton, 2019) as well as six books of prose about poetry. He lives in Granville, Ohio, teaches at Denison University, and curates the *Kenyon Review*'s annual eco-poetry feature "Nature's Nature."

SUSAN BARBA is the editor of *American Wildflowers: A Literary Field Guide,* which received the 2023 American Horticultural Society Book Award, and the author of the poetry collections *geode* and *Fair Sun.* She works as a senior editor for New York Review Books.

SARAH BARBER is author of *Country House,* winner of the 2017 Pleiades Press Editors Prize for Poetry, and *The Kissing Party,* published in 2010 by the National Poetry Review Press. Her poems appear widely, and she teaches at St. Lawrence University in Canton, New York.

ROBIN BECKER is the author of eight poetry collections, most recently *The Black Bear Inside Me* and *Tiger Heron,* both from University of Pittsburgh Press. She is professor emeritus at Penn State University. Among her many awards are the Lambda Literary Award and a fellowship from the National Endowment for the Arts.

LISA BELLAMY is the author of *The Northway* (Terrapin Books) and *Nectar,* a chapbook. She has received Pushcart and Fugue Poetry prizes. The UN Network on Migration featured her poem "Yoho" in a 2022 exhibition. She studies with Philip Schultz at the Writers Studio, where she also teaches.

SARAH BLAKE is the author of *In Springtime, Clean Air, Naamah, Let's Not Live on Earth,* and *Mr. West.* She received the National Jewish Book Award for Debut Fiction and a Literature Fellowship from the National Endowment for the Arts for her poetry.

DAVE BONTA is a web publisher (davebonta.com) best known for the poetry film site movingpoems.com. Print collections include *Ice Mountain* (Phoenicia Publishing, 2017) and *Breakdown: Banjo Poems* (Seven Kitchens Press, 2013). He lives in Tyrone, Pennsylvania, and his current writing obsessions include a project to make erasure poems from every entry in the *Diary of Samuel Pepys.*

ELIZABETH BRADFIELD's most recent books are *Toward Antarctica* and *Theorem.* She is coeditor of *Cascadia Field Guide: Art, Ecology, Poetry* and *Broadsided Press: Fifteen Years of Poetic/Artistic Collaboration.* Her work has appeared in the *Atlantic Monthly,* the *Sun,* and *Orion,* and her honors include the Audre Lorde Prize and a Stegner Fellowship. Liz lives on Cape Cod.

JOSEPH J. CAPISTA is the author of *Intrusive Beauty* (Ohio University Press, 2019). He has received awards from the National Endowment for the Humanities, the Maryland State Arts Council, and the Bread Loaf Writers' Conference. He teaches at Towson University and lives with his family in Baltimore.

STACIE CASSARINO's most recent collection of poems, *Each Luminous Thing*, won the Lexi Rudnitsky Editor's Choice Award with Persea Books. She is the author of *Zero at the Bone* (2009), which received a Lambda Literary Award and the Audre Lorde Award, and a monograph, *Culinary Poetics and Edible Images in 20C American Literature* (2018). She lives in Vermont with her three daughters.

GEORGE DAVID CLARK is the author of *Reveille*, winner of the Miller Williams Prize, and *Newly Not Eternal*, forthcoming from Louisiana State University Press. The editor of *32 Poems*, he is an associate professor of English at Washington and Jefferson College and lives in McMurray, Pennsylvania, with his wife and their four children.

GRANT CLAUSER is the author of several books, including *Muddy Dragon on the Road to Heaven*. His poems have appeared in *American Poetry Review*, *Greensboro Review*, *Kenyon Review*, and other journals. He camps, hikes, fishes, gardens, and works in Pennsylvania and teaches at Rosemont College.

J. L. CONRAD is the author of the full-length collection *A Cartography of Birds* (Louisiana State University Press) and the chapbooks *Recovery* (Texas Review Press) and *NOT IF BUT WHEN* (Salt Hill). Her poems have appeared in *Pleiades*, *Jellyfish*, *Sugar House Review*, *Salamander*, *Beloit Poetry Journal*, *Moon City Review*, and elsewhere.

GEFFREY DAVIS is the author of *Revising the Storm*, *Night Angler*, and a forthcoming third collection (all published by BOA Editions). A recipient of fellowships from Bread Loaf, Cave Canem, and the National Endowment for the Arts, Davis teaches for the University of Arkansas and the Rainier Writing Workshop.

ALISON HAWTHORNE DEMING was born and grew up in Connecticut, steeped in literary and naturalist traditions. She is the author of six books of poetry and five of nonfiction, most recently *A Woven World* (Counterpoint, 2021). She is Regents Professor Emerita at the University of Arizona.

CHARD DENIORD is the author of six books of poetry, most recently *In My Unknowing* (University of Pittsburgh Press, 2020) and *Interstate* (University of Pittsburgh Press, 2019). Professor emeritus of English and creative writing at Providence College, he serves as a board member of the Sundog Poetry Center in Vermont, is the essay editor at *Plume Poetry Journal*, and lives in Westminster West, Vermont, with his wife, Liz.

REBECCA FOUST's seventh book *ONLY* (Four Way Books, 2022) received a *Publisher's Weekly* starred review. Recognitions include runner-up for the 2022 *Missouri Review* Editors Prize; winner of the Pablo Neruda, C. P. Cavafy, and James Hearst poetry prizes; the Marin Poet Laureateship; and Hedgebrook, MacDowell, and Sewanee fellowships. New poems appear in the *Common*, *Ploughshares*, *POETRY*, and *Quarterly West*.

HANNAH FRIES is the author of the poetry collection *Little Terrarium* and a selection of writing and meditations called *Being with Trees*. Her work has appeared in *EcoTheo Review, Terrain.org, American Poetry Review*, and elsewhere. She grew up in New Hampshire and now lives with her family in western Massachusetts.

MICHAEL GARRIGAN writes and teaches along the Susquehanna River in Pennsylvania. He is the author of the poetry collections *River, Amen* and *Robbing the Pillars*. He served as an artist in residence for the Bob Marshall Wilderness Area and has written for *Orion* about what he calls the postindustrial wilderness.

ADAM GIANNELLI is the author of *Tremulous Hinge* (University of Iowa Press, 2017), winner of the Iowa Poetry Prize, and the translator of a selection of prose poems by Marosa di Giorgio, *Diadem* (BOA Editions, 2012).

MARGARET GIBSON served as poet laureate of Connecticut from 2019 to 2022. She is the author of thirteen books of poetry, most recently *Draw Me without Boundaries* and *The Glass Globe*. Her awards include a Lamont Selection, the Melville Kane Award, and the Connecticut Book Award. She edited *Waking Up to the Earth: Connecticut Poets in a Time of Global Climate Crisis*.

CHARITY GINGERICH's first collection of poems, *After June*, won the Hopper Poetry Prize (Green Writers Press, 2019). She was a Tennessee William's scholar at the Sewanee Writers Conference, and her work has appeared in such journals as *North American Review*, the *Kenyon Review*, *FIELD*, and *Tahoma Literary Review*.

ANDREW C. GOTTLIEB was born in Ontario, Canada, and grew up outside of Boston. He now lives in Irvine, California, and is the author of *Tales of a Distance* (Wandering Aengus Press, 2022). Poets whose work make up "Cento for Northern Pike" include Sandra Alcosser, F. Douglas Brown, Rob Carney, Wanda Coleman, Noah Davis, Todd Davis, Alison Hawthorne Deming, Mona Van Duyn, Nick Flynn, Jack Gilbert, Jim Harrison, Jill Osier, Emily Pérez, Carl Sandburg, Chris Santiago, Charlie Smith, Kay Ryan, and Joe Wilkins.

WILLARD P. GREENWOOD II is from Maine and lives in Hiram, Ohio. He has taught at Hiram College since 2001. He lives with his wife, Beth, and two sons Robert and Michael. His oldest son, Max, lives in Vermont. He teaches courses on writing, literature, and fly fishing.

JEFF GUNDY is Distinguished Poet-in-Residence at Bluffton University and has published thirteen books, including *Wind Farm: Landscape with Stories and Towers* (creative nonfiction) and *Without a Plea* and *Abandoned Homeland* (both poetry). A former Fulbright lecturer in Austria, he was named Ohio Poet of the Year for his book, *Somewhere Near Defiance*.

GARY HAWKINS's debut poetry collection, *Worker*, was published by Main Street Rag. His poems and essays have appeared in numerous journals. With his wife, the poet Landon Godfrey, he edits and produces *Croquet*, an occasional letterpress broadside delivered as a postcard. He lives in Northampton, Massachusetts.

K. A. HAYS is the author of four collections of poetry, most recently *Anthropocene Lullaby* (Carnegie Mellon, 2022). Her poems have appeared in *Best American Poetry* anthologies, *Orion* magazine, and elsewhere. She teaches in the creative writing program at Bucknell University and lives in Lewisburg, Pennsylvania.

JOHN HODGEN is writer-in-residence at Assumption University in Worcester, Massachusetts, and advisory editor for *New Letters* at the University of Missouri at Kansas City. Hodgen won the AWP Prize in Poetry for *Grace* (University of Pittsburgh Press, 2005). His sixth book, *What We May Be*, was published by Lynx House Press.

HENRY HUGHES grew up in New York and now teaches at Western Oregon University. He is an Oregon Book Award–winning poet; author of the memoir, *Back Seat with Fish*; and a frequent contributor to *Anglers Journal*, *Queen's Quarterly*, and *Harvard Review*.

M. J. IUPPA was the author of five full-length collections, most recently *The Weight of Air* from Kelsay Books. A chapbook of microfiction, *Rock. Paper. Scissors.*, was published by Foothills Publishing. For thirty-four years, she lived on a small farm near the shores of Lake Ontario. She passed away in April 2023.

JULIE SWARSTAD JOHNSON is the author of *Pennsylvania Furnace* and coeditor of *Beyond Earth's Edge: The Poetry of Spaceflight*. A graduate of Penn State's creative writing MFA program, she lives in Tucson, Arizona, and is an archivist and librarian at the University of Arizona Poetry Center.

KASEY JUEDS is the author of two collections of poetry, both from the University of Pittsburgh Press: *Keeper*, which won the 2012 Agnes Lynch Starrett Prize, and *The Thicket*. She lives in a small town in the mountains of New York State.

JULIA SPICHER KASDORF has published four books in the Pitt Poetry Series, most recently *As Is*. With photographer Steven Rubin, she wrote *Shale Play*, a documentary poetry project depicting the impacts of fracking in Pennsylvania. She teaches at Penn State and directs the creative writing program.

TALLEY V. KAYSER's poems and prose have appeared in the *Gettysburg Review*, *Cimarron Review*, *Alpinist*, and elsewhere. Her writing about animals has been recognized by PEN Northwest and the Center for American Literary Studies, as well as being nominated for a Pushcart Prize.

DANIEL LASSELL grew up in Kentucky and lives in New York with his wife and children. His first poetry collection, *Spit* (2021), won the Wheelbarrow Books Poetry Prize. He is also the author of two limited-edition chapbooks, *Ad Spot* (2021) and *The Emptying Earth* (2023).

SYDNEY LEA is a former Pulitzer finalist and served as founding editor of *New England Review*. He was Vermont's poet laureate from 2011 to 2015. A fifteenth collection of poems, *What Shines*, was published in 2023. In 2021, he was presented with his home state of Vermont's most prestigious artist's distinction: the Governor's Award for Excellence in the Arts.

DIANE LEBLANC is a writer, teacher, and book artist with roots in Vermont, Wyoming, and Minnesota. She is the author of *The Feast Delayed* (Terrapin Books, 2021) and four poetry chapbooks. Diane is a holistic life coach with emphasis in creativity practice, and she teaches writing at St. Olaf College.

XIAOLY LI received the Massachusetts Cultural Council Artist Fellowship Grant in Poetry in 2022. Her poetry collection, *Every Single Bird Rising*, was published by Future Cycle Press in 2023. She has been nominated for Best New Poets, twice for a Pushcart Prize, and three times for Best of the Net.

ANNI LIU was born in Xi'an, China, and is the author of *Border Vista* (Persea Books), a *New York Times* Best Poetry Book of 2022. Her work has been featured in *Poem-a-Day*, *Poetry*, the *Adroit Journal*, and elsewhere. She's an Undocupoets Fellow and edits prose at Graywolf Press.

MARJORIE MADDOX is professor of English at Commonwealth University in Pennsylvania. She has published fourteen poetry collections, most recently *Begin with a Question* (Iron Pen, 2022) and the ekphrastic collaborations, *Heart Speaks, Is Spoken For* and *In the Museum of My Daughter's Mind*, both from Shanti Arts. She also has published a story collection and four children's books.

KERRIN MCCADDEN is the author of *Landscape with Plywood Silhouettes* (New Issues, 2014), *Keep This to Yourself* (Button Poetry, 2020), and *American Wake* (Black Sparrow Press, 2021). She has received a National Endowment for the Arts fellowship and has won the Vermont Book Award and the Button Poetry Prize. McCadden teaches at the Center for Technology, Essex, and lives with her family in South Burlington, Vermont.

SHARA MCCALLUM, originally from Jamaica and born to a Jamaican father and Venezuelan mother, has published six books, including her most recent, *No Ruined Stone*, winner of the 2022 Hurston/Wright Legacy Award for Poetry. An anthology of her poems translated into Spanish by Adalber Salas Hernández, *La historia es un cuarto*, was published in 2021 in Mexico. McCallum is an Edwin Erle Sparks Professor of English at Penn State University, is on the faculty of the Pacific University Low-Residency MFA, and served as the 2021–22 Penn State laureate.

ABBY MINOR lives in the ridges and valleys of central Pennsylvania, where she works on poems, essays, gardens, and projects exploring reproductive politics. Her first book, *As I Said: A Dissent* (Ricochet Editions, 2022), is a collection of long documentary poems concerning abortion, embodiment, justice, and citizenship in U.S. history.

ROGER MITCHELL is the author of twelve books of poetry, most recently *Reason's Dream* (Dos Madres, 2018). His collection of reviews and essays, *Their Own Society: Prose on Poetry*, was published by Hamilton Stone Editions in 2022. He has completed a biography of the poet Jean Garrigue. He lives in Jay, New York, with his wife, the fiction writer, Dorian Gossy.

NIK MOORE is a Kentucky poet and University of Montana MFA graduate whose work appears in *GASHER*, *Olney*, *Moon Cola*, and elsewhere. Nik likes roaming around the woods and waters of southern Ohio with their niece and nephews.

AIMEE NEZHUKUMATATHIL is the author of the nature essay collection, *World of Wonders*, and four books of poems. She is professor of English in the MFA program at the University of Mississippi and poetry editor of the Sierra Club's *SIERRA* magazine.

LEAH POOLE OSOWSKI is the author of *hover over her* (Kent State University Press, 2016), winner of the Wick Poetry Prize, and *Exceeds Us* (Saturnalia, 2023), winner of the Alma Award. Her work has appeared in the *Southern Review*, the *Georgia Review*, *Gettysburg Review*, and elsewhere.

SEAN PRENTISS is the author of *Finding Abbey: The Search for Edward Abbey and His Hidden Desert Grave*, which won the National Outdoor Book Award, and *Crosscut: Poems*. He cowrote two textbooks, *Environmental and Nature Writing* and *Advanced Creative Nonfiction*. He serves as associate professor at Norwich University. He and his family live in northern Vermont.

L. RENÉE is a poet and nonfiction writer living in Harrisonburg, Virginia. She works as assistant director of Furious Flower Poetry Center and assistant professor of English at James Madison University. Her award-winning work has been published in *Obsidian*, *Rattle*, *Tin House Online*, *Appalachian Review*, *Poetry Northwest*, and elsewhere.

JACK RIDL grew up in Pennsylvania and later taught for several decades at Hope College, where he was named Michigan Professor of the Year by the Carnegie Foundation. He is the author of many books, including *Saint Peter and the Goldfinch*, *Practicing to Walk Like a Heron*, and *Broken Symmetry*, all published by Wayne State University Press. Among his honors are the ForeWord Magazine Book of the Year Gold Medal, the Society of Midland Authors award, and the NYC Center for Book Arts Award.

CHRISTINA SEYMOUR is the author of *When Is a Burning Tree* (Glass Lyre Press) and *Flowers around Your Soft Throat* (Structo). Her work appears in *Raleigh Review*, *Blood Tree Literature*, the *Moth*, *North American Review*, *Cimarron Review*, Wick Poetry Center's *Speak Peace: American Voices Respond to Vietnamese Children's Paintings*, and elsewhere.

NEIL SHEPARD is the author of several poetry collections, most recently *How It Is: Selected Poems* (Salmon Poetry, 2018) and *The Book of Failures* (Madville Publishing, 2024). He edited *Green Mountains Review* for a quarter century and currently edits the online magazine *Plant-Human Quarterly*. He splits his time between Vermont and New York City.

JULIA SHIPLEY is an arts and culture journalist and investigative reporter whose creative work has appeared in *AGNI*, *Gettysburg Review*, *Plume*, *Orion*, and *Poetry*. Her debut collection, *The Academy of Hay*, won the Melissa Lanitis Gregory Award. Her second collection, *An Animal inside an Animal*, was a finalist for the Mura Award and Hecht Prize and is forthcoming from Tinderbox Press.

BETSY SHOLL's tenth collection of poetry is *As If a Song Could Save You* (University of Wisconsin, 2022), winner of the Four Lakes Prize. She teaches in the MFA writing program of Vermont College of Fine Arts and served as poet laureate of Maine from 2006 to 2011.

DAVID SHUMATE is the author of three books of prose poems published by the University of Pittsburgh Press: *Kimonos in the Closet* (2013), *The Floating Bridge* (2008), and *High Water Mark* (2004).

MATTHEW J. SPIRENG lives on a wooded acreage left from the family farm in the foothills of the eastern Catskills. His 2019 Sinclair Poetry Prize–winning book, *Good Work,* was published by Evening Street Press. An eleven-time Pushcart Prize nominee, he is author of two other full-length poetry books and five chapbooks.

ELEANOR STANFORD is the author of three books of poems. Her work has appeared in *Poetry, Ploughshares, Harvard Review,* the *Iowa Review,* and many others. She was a Fulbright fellow to Brazil and the recipient of a 2019 National Endowment for the Arts grant in poetry. She lives in the Philadelphia area.

JORDAN TEMCHACK, the hillbillibrettist-bard of Central Pennsylkrainia, orchestrates *Rumble & Scream*—a folk-rock opera with a backwoods family band. He produces and engineers postindustrial mountain music at the Noise Shack. His poetry has been published in *Northern Appalachia Review, Prime Number Magazine,* and *Passengers Journal.*

PHILIP TERMAN's most recent books are *This Crazy Devotion* (Broadstone, 2020), *Our Portion: New and Selected Poems* (Autumn House, 2015), and, as cotranslator, *Tango Beneath a Narrow Ceiling: The Selected Poems of Riad Saleh Hussein* (Bitter Oleander, 2021). He directs the Bridge Literary Arts Center in Franklin, Pennsylvania.

CHASE TWICHELL is the author of eight books of poetry, most recently *Things as It Is* (Copper Canyon, 2018). Her new and selected *Horses Where the Answers Should Have Been* (Copper Canyon, 2010) won both the Kingsley Tufts Award and the Balcones Poetry Prize. She splits the year between the Adirondacks and Saratoga Springs.

LEE UPTON's most recent book is *The Day Every Day Is* (Saturnalia, 2023). Her poetry has appeared widely, including in the *New Yorker, Poetry,* the *Southern Review,* and three editions of *Best American Poetry.* She is a fiction writer and literary critic as well as a poet.

JUDITH VOLLMER's sixth book of poetry, *The Sound Boat: New and Selected Poems,* was awarded the 2022 University of Wisconsin Press Four Lakes Prize. She is recipient of fellowships from the National Endowment for the Arts, Pennsylvania Council on the Arts, the Corporation of Yaddo, and the American Academy in Rome.

RYAN WALSH is author of the poetry collection *Reckonings* (2019). He grew up next to the Monongahela National Forest in West Virginia and has made his home in mountain areas from western North Carolina to northern Vermont. He now lives in Pittsburgh, Pennsylvania, and walks daily in the 644-acre woods at the end of the street.

HENRY WALTERS is the author of two collections of poetry, most recently *The Nature Thief* (Waywiser, 2022), a finalist for the Anthony Hecht Poetry Prize. He lives in New Hampshire with his young family, two hawks, and a hive of bees.

JERRY WEMPLE has published three poetry collections and has a new collection forthcoming. He grew up in the Ridge and Valley section of Pennsylvania. After a stint in the U.S. Navy and working as a reporter, he returned to the Keystone State. He teaches at Bloomsburg University.

KAREN J. WEYANT's poems have been published in *Chautauqua, Crab Orchard Review, Copper Nickel, Lake Effect, Poetry East, Spillway, Rattle,* and *River Styx*. A resident of Warren, Pennsylvania, she is an associate professor of English at Jamestown Community College in Jamestown, New York.

JOE WILKINS is the author of the novel, *Fall Back Down When I Die*; a memoir, *The Mountain and the Fathers*; and four collections of poetry, including *When We Were Birds* and *Thieve*. Wilkins and his family spent a year living in the north country of New York when he served as Viebranz Visiting Professor of Creative Writing at St. Lawrence University. He is a professor of English at Linfield University in western Oregon.

Artists

EMILY BEAM earned degrees in biology and visual arts from Penn State Altoona. Her work consists of paintings and mixed media pieces that utilize nontraditional objects. She received the Zoller and Fine Arts Awards from Penn State University. Her art has been featured at the Southern Alleghenies Museum of Art and used in mammalian anatomy classes.

JOE BEAM is a visual artist from Bellwood, Pennsylvania. He earned a bachelor of fine arts from Penn State University in 2021. He works in a colorful, animated palette and loves to bend perspective and reality within his images.

ALLYSON COMSTOCK is professor emerita at Auburn University. Her artwork has been supported by a National Science Foundation Antarctic Artists and Writers Grant, fellowships from the Women's Studio Workshop, and residencies at Ucross Foundation and the Hambidge Center. Comstock's artwork has been exhibited at the Czong Institute for Contemporary Art in South Korea, the Ohio Craft Museum, and the Delaware Contemporary Art Center.

ROBERTO D'AMANDA is a mixed media artist from upstate New York and based in Baltimore, Maryland. Her work is primarily focused on history, archiving, and the creation of a personal symbology. She is currently pursuing a master of arts in teaching at the Maryland Institute College of Art.

ASHLEY HAMERSMA is a botanical illustrator and paleobotanist. She has a fondness for Midwest and Southeast flora and enjoys exploring nature and the way that people connect to plants through art. Her paleobotanical interests include morphometrics, floristic disjunction, and North American vegetation change through the Mesozoic.

GARY HAWKINS is a visual artist whose drawings and illustrations have appeared in multiple galleries and publications. He serves as vice president for academic affairs and dean of faculty at Hampshire College in Amherst, Massachusetts.

TALLEY V. KAYSER makes portraits of animals using wood, charcoal, and wax—most often in collaboration with her partner, David. This is Talley's first publication of visual art.

GWEN NOLL grew up backpacking the Appalachian Trail and exploring the mountains of the State College area in Pennsylvania, where she spent much of her childhood. Being raised by a family of artists gave her the ability to preserve memories of the beloved wildlife from her childhood on paper.

RAY NOLL discovered pen and ink as a child by studying the animal drawings of Ned Smith in *Pennsylvania Game News*. Graduating with an art degree from Penn State University, Ray worked as a book and magazine graphic designer/illustrator in Washington, D.C. He has exhibited nationally and internationally for five decades. Ray currently has studios in Valdosta, Georgia, and Siena, Italy.

HENRY SHEARON is an artist currently living in Raleigh, North Carolina. A graduate of Warren Wilson College, he works with mediums including pen and ink and various forms of print making and textiles. He has a great appreciation for the outdoors and gathers much of his inspiration from nature.

QUINLIN TAYLOR is a nonbinary artist from northwestern Maryland. Having started to draw because of a love for Earth's natural history, she briefly studied abstract painting at the Maryland Institute College of Art before leaving to pursue other ventures. She now finds an outlet in her independent practice.

Scientists

SARAH E. ALLEN earned a BS in geoscience from Hobart and William Smith Colleges in Geneva, New York, and a PhD in botany from the University of Florida. She completed a postdoc at Florissant Fossil Beds National Monument in Colorado. Dr. Allen's research is in paleobotany and associated disciplines. She has studied Cretaceous and Cenozoic plant fossils from Montana, Wyoming, Colorado, and Peru. Her work has been published in various journals, including *American Journal of Botany*, *International Journal of Plant Sciences*, and *Palaeogeography, Palaeoclimatology, Palaeoecology*. She is a faculty member in the Biology Department at Penn State Altoona.

CARL ENGSTROM graduated from the Pennsylvania State University with a BS in biology and a minor in wildlife and fisheries science. He grew up in central Pennsylvania and has been fascinated by birds his entire life and is working to pursue his passion professionally. He has assisted with academic avian research in a variety of species and settings, including on several projects in the Appalachians. Currently, he is a graduate student at the Ohio State University, researching the long-term impacts of silvicultural practices on cerulean warbler breeding dynamics.

JERRY D. HASSINGER, a veteran, has an MS from Penn State University and a BS from the University of Montana, worked in four National Parks, collected mammals in Afghanistan for the Field Museum of Natural History in Chicago, spent two years working for the Iran Game and Fish Department, was the Pennsylvania Bureau of Forestry's first wildlife biologist, and after eight years transferred to the Pennsylvania Game Commission to help launch a wildlife diversity and endangered species program. Retired since 2002, Jerry is current chair of the Pennsylvania Biological Survey's Mycological and Protists Technical Committee.

ANDREW L. SHIELS is a retired deputy executive director of the Pennsylvania Fish and Boat Commission. He holds an MS in biology from Shippensburg University and a BS in biology from Penn State University. His specialties include fish, reptiles and amphibians, endangered and threatened species, inland freshwater and coastal mid-Atlantic fisheries management, fish passage and migratory fishes, and natural resource policy and administration. He is a Certified Fisheries Professional Emeritus of the American Fisheries Society and former president of the Pennsylvania chapter. He has authored numerous popular and scientific articles and book chapters and served as editor on publications of noted species and topics.

HANNAH L. (CAVE) STOUT is a freelance conservation entomologist and a freshwater macroinvertebrate taxonomist certified by the Society for Freshwater Science. For her work on mayfly conservation, she earned a PhD in entomology from Penn State University. Her primary research focuses on invertebrate biodiversity of utility and transportation rights-of-way, and her specialties include identification of aquatic insects, wild bees, potter wasps, and ground beetles. Dr. Stout served on the boards of the Friends of the Frost Entomological Museum at Penn State University and the Keystone Water Resources Center. She currently serves on the board of the Association of Mid-Atlantic Aquatic Biologists.

Editors

TODD DAVIS lives between the villages of Bellwood and Tipton along the Allegheny Front in Pennsylvania where he spends much of his time in forty-one thousand acres of state game lands, observing the flora and fauna, foraging and fishing and hunting. He is the author of eight full-length collections of poetry—*Ditch Memory: New & Selected Poems*, *Coffin Honey*, *Native Species*, *Winterkill*, *In the Kingdom of the Ditch*, *The Least of These*, *Some Heaven*, and *Ripe*—as well as of a limited-edition chapbook, *Household of Water, Moon, and Snow*. He edited the nonfiction collection *Fast Break to Line Break: Poets on the Art of Basketball* and coedited the anthology *Making Poems*. His writing has won the Midwest Book Award, the Gwendolyn Brooks Poetry Prize, the Chautauqua Editors Prize, the Bloomsburg University Book Prize, and the Foreword INDIES Book of the Year Silver and Bronze Awards. His poems appear in such noted journals and magazines as *American Poetry Review*, *Alaska Quarterly Review*, *Iowa Review*, *North American Review*, *Missouri Review*, *Gettysburg Review*, *Orion*, *Poetry Northwest*, *Prairie Schooner*, *Southern Humanities Review*, and *Poetry Daily*. He teaches environmental studies, creative writing, and American literature at Penn State Altoona.

NOAH DAVIS grew up at the base of the Allegheny Front in Pennsylvania, where he learned the ecology of his home. His poetry collection, *Of This River*, was selected by George Ella Lyon for the 2019 Wheelbarrow Emerging Poet Book Prize from Michigan State University's Center for Poetry, and his second book, *The Last Beast We Revel In*, is forthcoming from CavanKerry Press. His poems and prose have appeared in the *Sun*, *Southern Humanities Review*, *Best New Poets*, *Orion*, the *Year's Best Sports Writing*, *North*

American Review, and *River Teeth*, among others. Davis earned his MFA from Indiana University, and his work has been awarded a Katharine Bakeless Nason Fellowship at the Bread Loaf Writers Conference and the 2018 Jean Ritchie Appalachian Literature Fellowship from Lincoln Memorial University. He works for the Theodore Roosevelt Conservation Partnership.

CAROLYN G. MAHAN, professor of biology and environmental studies at Penn State Altoona, holds a PhD in wildlife science from Penn State University and a BS in natural resources management engineering from the University of Connecticut. Research interests include biodiversity in threatened ecosystems, effects of human-modified landscapes on wildlife, and behavioral ecology of mammals. Her work has been published in *Conservation Biology*, *Journal of Mammalogy*, and *PLOS One*, among others. Dr. Mahan served on the boards of Pennsylvania Wildlife Society, Pennsylvania Center for Private Forests, and is past president of Pennsylvania Biological Survey. She currently serves on Governor Shapiro's Advisory Council for Conservation in Pennsylvania.

Credits for Artwork

All artwork was commissioned for this volume. The artists and their respective works are as follows:

Emily Beam: "New England Aster" and "Tessellated Darter."

Joe Beam: "Northern Dusky Salamander," "Northern Ring-necked Snake," "Fallfish," "Landlocked Salmon," and "Puffball."

Allyson Comstock: "Chestnut Oak," "Striped Maple," "White Pine," "Belted Kingfisher," "Red-eyed Vireo," "Eastern Milk Snake," "Pickerel Frog," "Wood Frog," "Eastern Blacknose Dace," "Common Eastern Firefly," and "Chicken of the Woods."

Roberto D'Amanda: "Common Loon," "Miner Bee," and "Monarch Butterfly."

Ashley Hamersma: "Black Birch," "Hobblebush," "Teaberry," and "Turkey Tail."

Gary Hawkins: "Balsam Fir," "Blue-stemmed Goldenrod," "Wood Sorrel," "Porcupine," "Dark-eyed Junco," "Red-backed Salamander," "Wood Turtle," "American Shad," "Northern Pike," and "Crown-tipped Coral."

Talley V. Kayser: "Hairy Woodpecker" and "Northern Goshawk."

Gwen Noll: "Mink."

Ray Noll: "American Beech," "Black Cherry," "Shagbark Hickory," "Allegheny Blackberry," "Mayapple," "Beaver," "Black Bear," "Bobcat," "Eastern Chipmunk," "Fisher," "Moose," "Red Squirrel," "Snowshoe Hare," "White-tailed Deer," "Bald Eagle," "Black-capped Chickadee," "Great Horned Owl," and "Brook Trout."

Henry Shearon: "Allegheny Serviceberry," "Bluebead Lily," "Jewelweed," "Hermit Thrush," "American Eel," "American Carrion Beetle," "Cecropia Moth," "Eastern Elliptio Mussel," "American Golden Chanterelle," "Scarlet Elf Cup," and "Yellow Morel."

Quinlin Taylor: "Common Five-lined Skink," "Chain Pickerel," and "Appalachian Brook Crayfish."